WORTHWHILE STRUGGLE

Patrick McCaskey

A Sports and Faith Series Book

ISBN: 978-0-9819342-4-2

Sporting Chance Press™, Inc.
1074 Butler Drive, Crystal Lake, IL 60014
sportingchancepress.com

Photographs and illustrations appearing in *Worthwhile Struggle* were sourced from: Associated Press; Challenged Atheletes Foundation; Curt Rabinak; Daniel Norris; Fr. Burke Masters; Fr. Kyle Manno; Fr. Lawrence Lew, O.P.; Frank Faunce; General Mills; John Malham of Trinity Icons; Lawndale Community Church; Loyola Academy Wilmette; Loyola University Chicago; Notre Dame Prep Niles; Wheaton College; Wikipedia (Fredrik L. Magnusson, Herbert Mason of the Daily Mail, Monday Night Football, National Portrait Gallery of London); and William Potter.

Please see the Photographs and Illustrations Credit Table on pages 310-313 for more information.

The opinions and ideas expressed are those of the author who is entirely responsible for its content. The author has composed *Worthwhile Struggle* at his own expense, using his own resources and technology. This publication is not associated in any way with the Chicago Bears Football Team.

"St. Kevin and the Blackbird" from OPENED GROUND: SELECTED POEMS, 1966-1996 by Seamus Heaney. Copyright © 1998 by Seamus Heaney. Reprinted by permission of Farrar, Straus and Giroux.

Worthwhile Struggle is Book 4 of the Sports and Faith Series.

Committee work is a worthwhile struggle.

Family is a worthwhile struggle.

Football is a worthwhile struggle.

Love is a worthwhile struggle.

Providing respectful comic relief is a worthwhile struggle.

Writing books is a worthwhile struggle.

INTRODUCTION

When I was seven months in my mother's womb, she received the blessing for expectant mothers. When my parents brought me home from the hospital, the lilacs in the side yard were in beautiful full bloom.

I started going to Bears' games when I was five. My brothers and I sat on an army blanket next to the Bears' bench while my grandfather coached. My grandfather once said to an official, "No man is completely worthless. You can always serve as a horrible example."

I started going to Bears' training camps when I was seven. George Blanda taught us how to kick. Bill George taught us how to play linebacker. Bill Wade taught us how to play quarterback.

When I was a high school senior, I was on a football team that won every game by an average of 29 points. After high school, my eye doctor said to me, "No more contact sports."

In 1974, I started working for the Bears. In 1981, the Bears had a half mile run to start training camp. One player, Kris Haines, finished ahead of me. He was later cut.

In 1982, the Bears had a mile and a half run to start training camp. After I had finished first, Walter Payton said to me, "I tried to stay with you. Then I said, 'That boy is crazy.'" That made all the training worthwhile.

For my 33rd birthday, I received permission to date. After nine months of prayer, I met Gretchen through mutual friends. Four months later, we looked at a house that was for sale. After the tour, Gretchen asked me, "Why are you looking for a house?"

I crossed my mouth with the back of my right hand and muttered, "In case you want to get married." She accepted my invitation.

We have been blessed with three sons: Ed, Tom, and Jim. They were named after my father and his brothers in the same birth order.

In 2003, I had a right corneal transplant. In 2004, I had a left corneal transplant. My eyes are fine now, but I still can't play for the Bears.

I left the swing set up on purpose because I was hoping for grandchildren. I was mocked and scorned. Now that I am a grandfather, I'm a man of vision: Christopher Columbus, the Wright brothers, Pat McCaskey.

Mitch Trubisky is wearing my number.

The Ten Commandments of Football

I.   Football is a wonderful game. There's blocking and tackling and much, much more. Be enthusiastic.

II. Weddings, births, and vacations should take place during the off-seasons.

III. Remember the Hupmobile and the original meeting.

IV. All previous games are preparation for the next one.

V.   Obey the personal conduct policy.

VI. Work for the good of the league.

VII. Win championships with sportsmanship.

VIII. You shall not criticize the officials.

IX. You shall not covet other teams' coaches or players.

X.   Game times are tentative and subject to flexible scheduling.

– Contents –

SISTER JEAN AND LOYOLA RAMBLERS

FOOTBALL IS A WONDERFUL GAME. THERE'S BLOCKING AND TACKLING AND MUCH, MUCH MORE. BE ENTHUSIASTIC.

INTRODUCTION

Sports and Faith is a *calling* for my family. Faith is the beacon that guides us and football is what we do. They are inseparable for us. My mother recites the Rosary on navy blue and burnt orange beads when she travels with the team. My grandfather broke the huddle at the Chicago Bears' office on Saturdays to go to Confession at Saint Peter's in the Loop. He returned to his desk to say his penance. There are Masses and chapel services on game days for our players and staff.[1] We don't apologize for our love of faith or football.

My grandfather was enthusiastic about professional football, which was his vocation and is mine today. The meaning of the first football commandment is ***honor and love what you do.***

SISTER JEAN DOLORES SCHMIDT, BVM

Few people live as long as Sister Jean or love what they do with such passion. Sister Jean is one of a kind.

Four laywomen started a school for girls in Dublin, Ireland, in 1832. In the following year, the women immigrated to Philadelphia and began teaching children of Irish immigrants. A religious congregation was created as the Sisters of Charity of the Blessed Virgin Mary. A second location was established to serve a pioneer community outside of Dubuque at the invitation of Bishop Mathias Loras. It became the BVM's first Motherhouse, St. Joseph on the Prairie. About 50 years later a new motherhouse was built along the bluffs of the Mississippi called Mount Carmel.[2]

Roughly 5,000 members of the order have joined since the beginnings of the first School in Dublin. One of the 5,000 is Sister Jean Dolores Schmidt who is known widely today as Sister Jean of Loyola University. After teaching for 20 years in elementary schools and coaching girls' basketball, volleyball, softball, and track at schools in the Chicago and Los Angeles areas, Sister Jean took a job at the Catholic all-women's Mundelein College near Loyola's campus in the Rogers Park neighborhood of Chicago in 1961. Mundelein was folded into Loyola University in 1991 and Sister Jean continued to serve but without a formal position at Loyola. In 2007, her BVM convent was sold to the University and Sister was being sent back to the motherhouse in Iowa. But the then-President of Loyola, Father Michael J. Garanzini, didn't want to lose her—she was a great presence even though she was in her late 80s! He made arrangements to hire her on and provide housing. Sister Jean has been an academic advisor, campus minister, and chaplain to the men's basketball team—along with other assorted duties.

Part of Sister's duties has her focused on team members' education and personal development. Sister Jean also scouts opposing teams and has delivered scouting reports to Head Coach Porter Moser.[3] Sister Jean is only 5-foot tall, but happy to work with young athletes and students. The articulate, young-sounding 99-year-old woman is a media sensation who has created positive energy along with the Loyola athletes, coaches, and fans. During the 2018 NCAA Basketball Tournament, Sister Jean received national attention as the team continued on a path of upsets and nail-biters.

SISTER JEAN QUOTES

"I love being with people, spreading God's word. And you do that not by talking all the time, but just by your presence."

"Bopping around the sidelines in my Nikes and trifocals, standing 5 feet tall, I'm towered over by the athletes, but they treat me like a queen."

On joining the convent:

"I was armed with one suitcase…and a sense of possibility."

On young people:

"I learn every day. My vocabulary has changed over the years by virtue of the fact that they use words differently. Everything is awesome, everything is cool."

"All you have to do is spend one day with the students here at Loyola and you'll be filled with great hope for the church."

On Pope Francis:

"And I'm excited by Pope Francis, not just because he's a Jesuit, but because he's asking us to evangelize, to share our faith with other people and listen to their faith as well. He needs our help. We better give it to him! He keeps telling us, 'God loves us. We may get tired of loving God, but He never gets tired of loving us.' To me that's a great gift."4

Our world, which includes the world of college basketball, is a better place since Sister Jean has graced it.

Loyola University Finishes in Final Four

A classic sports story unfolded in college basketball in 2018 with the Loyola Ramblers climbing to the NCAA Tournament's Final Four. The Ramblers' athletes and coaches succeeded on teamwork with discipline and inspiration. The Loyola season surprised almost all basketball fans, writers, and analysts, but nothing seemed to surprise the teams' players and coaches. Led by Head Coach Porter Moser, they took a one-game at-a-time approach.

The excitement increased with each game in the NCAA Basketball tournament. A different Loyola player stepped up in dramatic fashion in their team-first approach. Coach Moser and coaches Bryan Mullins, Drew Valentine, Matt Gordon along with Director of Basketball Operations, Jevon Mamon, and Graduate Assistant, London Dokubo, all guided the Ramblers to their most successful year since the 1963 National Championship.[5]

Donte Ingram, Marques Townes, Clayton Custer, Ben Richardson, Cameron Krutwig, Aundre Jackson, Lucas Williamson, Jake Baughman, Bruno Skokna, Adarius Avery, Christian Negron, Cameron Satterwhite, Dylan Boehm, Carson Shanks, Nick Dinardi, and Aher Uguak formed a Chicago powerhouse.[6]

In tournament games, Loyola won three games in a row on last minute buzzer beaters by three different players. First, in the Ramblers tournament opener on March 15, Donte Ingram popped a long 3-pointer at the top of the key with 1.6 seconds remaining to beat Miami, 64–62. Second, on Saint Patrick's Day, hounded by two defenders, Clayton Custer took a last-second shot against Tennessee that bounced around the rim in heart-breaking fashion before finally falling in for a 63–62 win. Third, on March 22, it was Marques Townes, who hit a towering 3-pointer from the side against Nevada with six seconds remaining that sealed it for the Ramblers, who went on to win, 69–68.

In the Elite eight matchup, Loyola beat Kansas State, 78-62, on March 24. But the season came to an end for the Ramblers on March 31 when they lost to the University of Michigan in a final four matchup, 69-57. Loyola had a cold day, only making 10-percent of its 3 pointers.

This highly disciplined Loyola team took inspiration from Sister Jean Dolores Smith, the 99-year old team chaplain and unofficial scout. The team achieved a 32-6 mark. In addition to all the team's and players' accolades, many point to the program as a new standard bearer for college programs that foster the good.

Both the coaches and players know that in some ways the Ramblers changed the college landscape this year with a team that could win big by playing well and playing with the right attitude. Ramblers are reminding fans that they may have taken people by surprise this year, but the talent was there.

Among many other accolades, Loyola's Basketball Team received the Sports Faith International College Team of the Year award.

CHIP BECK

At the young age of 10 years, Chip Beck's mother introduced him to golf by taking him to a junior clinic. He fell in love with the game. Beck's large Catholic family would include 10 kids, so taking kids to any outside activity must have been a challenge. Little did Mrs. Beck know the impact that sacrifice would make years later.

Beck enrolled at the University of Georgia where he became one of the most decorated golfers in the University's history. As a three-time All-American, five-time tournament winner, and with more top ten finishes than any other player in the school's history, Beck decided it was time to test his skills with the best players in the world on the PGA tour.

Beck has won four PGA Tour victories, and he has had twenty runner-up finishes. He won the Vardon Trophy in 1989 and he spent 40 weeks in the top 10 of the World Golf Rankings from 1988 through 1989.[7]

Prior to the Las Vegas Invitational, the Hilton family announced that anybody who could shoot 59 would be awarded a million dollars. Despite never having seen the course before, Beck had 5 pars and 13 birdies (a PGA Tour record for birdies in one round) including a three footer on the 18th hole to shoot a 59. He was the second player to ever shoot a 59 in a PGA tournament.[8]

Beck finished with a tie for third in the tournament, but half of the million dollars he won was used to fund the Chip Beck Scholarship. It's a gift that keeps on giving.

Many golf fans remember his superb round of 59 and other accomplishments, but ask him, and he will tell you he is just another guy who loves God, his family, and the game of golf.

The Beck family was a product of Catholic education. Chip's youngest sister was named after one of the nuns who taught the Beck children. Beck is a grateful athlete, who likes to point out that his wife ran the home most of the time so that Chip could make a living in professional golf. Beck was inducted into the Sports Faith Hall of Fame in 2016.[9]

LETTER FROM BOB COUSY

The "Houdini of the Hardwood," Bob Cousy, worked his magic for the Boston Celtics from 1950-1963. An NBA All-Star every season he played, Cousy's play initiated a love affair between Boston and its Celtics that continues to this day. The 6-foot-1 Cousy played guard like he had eyes in the back of his head—one of the game's best passers. He regularly used the behind-the-back dribble. "Cooz" revolutionized pro basketball in the 1950s with his sleight-of-hand play. He scored 50 points in one game—had 28 assists in another. Cousy was inducted into the Basketball Hall of Fame. ESPN named him one of the greatest athletes of 20th Century North America.[10]

With Cousy, one of the greatest basketball players of his era, the Celtics won six NBA Championships. Cousy and his wife, Marie, raised their two daughters with a strong sense of social justice and a passion for civil rights.[11] We honored his achievements and his great example of Catholic manhood by inducting him into the Sports Faith International Hall of Fame.[12] I sent Bob my book called *Pilgrimage* and he responded with the letter below:

Dear Pat-

Thank you for including me on your "Book of the Month Club" list 'Bears' on Pilgrimage, enjoyed it very much.

Pilgrimage brought back some very warm and personal memories for me—In the 50s I introduced my Jewish coach Red Auerbach to Fatima—during our working visit to Portugal—He didn't convert but he was very impressed with the commitment of the faithful.

Then in early 60s I brought my family to Lourdes for a visit (my daughters were about 10 + 11) followed by a week in Rome where we met someone who would become a lifelong friend and mentor to all of us, Father John Ed. Brooks S.J.

Father was studying in Rome, took the week off, had all his meals with us and acted as our guide for the entire time. Needless to say it made "The Eternal City" come alive for the four of us and turned it into a lifelong "happening." (He knows where all the bodies were buried—excuse the pun).

From there we returned to States where I started my six year coaching stint at Boston College and Father returned to Holy Cross where he eventually became President for 23 years. His name was put on one of our buildings last year—well deserved because in 1968 he opened the school to the African American student—very controversial and a book was written about it, since early students have become very successful, e.g. Ted Wells and Clarence Thomas.

Followed that up in 75 or 4 by allowing students with "skirts." Believe it or not this was even more controversial—am sorry to say both my daughters missed by 2 or 3 years. (Marie, who you spoke to, graduated B.C.) We buried Father 5 or 6 years ago at the Cathedral of the Holy Cross with 30 co-celebrants on the altar—most giants in the Catholic community.

At this point in my life, reliving those moments become more meaningful than the 6 N.B.A. Championships. So thanks again for lighting that spark.

I'm computer illiterate so excuse the scribbling—wish I could provide a "translator."

Peace,

Bob

Reverend John E. Brooks

Sports analysts write about coaching trees. People are affected by those who touch their lives. Bob Cousy loved and honored Father John E. Brooks.

Father Brooks, S.J. was the 29th President of the College of the Holy Cross, serving from 1970-1994. Under Brooks, New England's oldest Catholic college became coeducational and attracted a diverse student body. Brooks helped strengthen Holy Cross financially, energize the alumni, and built one of the country's top liberal arts institutions. His leadership to recruit African-American students at Holy Cross was chronicled in the book *Fraternity* by Diane Brady.

Born on July 13, 1923, in Dorchester, Massachusetts, Father Brooks entered Holy Cross in 1942. After taking time to serve in the U.S. Army in World War II, he returned to Holy Cross and graduated in 1949. He entered the New England Province of the Society of Jesus in 1950 and was ordained a priest on June 13, 1959, by Richard Cardinal Cushing of Boston.

Following the death of Martin Luther King Jr. in April of 1968, Father Brooks traveled to high schools along the East Coast to recruit African-American students to attend Holy Cross. These included Clarence Thomas, the Supreme Court justice; Edward P. Jones, Pulitzer Prize winner; Theodore Wells, one of the nation's most successful defense attorneys; Stanley Grayson, New York City deputy mayor who broke the color bar on Wall Street; and public servant and lawyer, Eddie Jenkins, who played for the Miami Dolphins during their 1972 perfect season.

Father Brooks helped found what has become the Patriot League, originally begun as a Division I football league, now expanded to be inclusive of all sports and to this day recognized for its promotion of high academic achievement among participating student-athletes. Father Brooks's friend and Holy Cross trustee, Jacob Hiatt, along with his daughter and son-in-law, Myra and Robert Kraft (New England Patriots), made a major gift to Holy Cross to endow a professorship.[13]

PASTOR WAYNE ("COACH") GORDON

COACH WAYNE GORDON

You won't often see Coach Wayne Gordon's name in the headlines or his face on television. And yet, he has been one of Chicago's movers and shakers for over 40 years. But Coach Gordon isn't about pulling political strings for his own sake or his friends. He is about selflessly helping others get a fair shake, helping others succeed, helping others build their own healthy community, and helping others to live faithfully. The Coach, as he likes to be called, is about coaching others to do what needs to be done.

Coach Wayne Gordon is my long-time family friend and a minister. Raised in Fort Dodge, Iowa, Gordon graduated from Wheaton College in 1975. He moved into the Lawndale Community after finishing school at Wheaton College and within a few years, he and a group of people in the neighborhood started the Lawndale Community Church. Coach Gordon and others established the Lawndale Christian Development Center and the Lawndale Christian Health Center. Coach Gordon gets high marks for creating indigenous leaders in the community. His "coaching tree" is long and impressive!

I spent some time with Coach Gordon and his wife Anne at their residence in Lawndale when I was young. He took me under his wing and taught me how to date using Biblical principles. I spoke at the Church's Fortieth Anniversary.[14]

Forty Years Lawndale Community Church

Forty has Biblical significance.

From Genesis 7:14, we know that the Lord said to Noah: *"Seven days from now I will bring rain down on the earth for forty days and forty nights, and so I will wipe out from the surface of the earth every moving creature that I have made."*

From Exodus 16:35, we know that, *"The Israelites ate this manna for forty years, until they came to settled land; they ate manna until they reached the borders of Canaan."*

From Exodus 24:18, we know that, *"Moses passed into the midst of the cloud as he went up on the mountain; and there he stayed for forty days and forty nights."*

From Matthew 4:2, we know that, *"Jesus fasted for forty days and forty nights, and afterwards he was hungry."*

Lawndale Lou Malnati's Pizzeria had not been invented yet.[15]

From Acts 1:3, we know that, *"Jesus presented himself alive to them by many proofs after he had suffered, appearing to them during forty days and speaking about the kingdom of God."*

Wall of Fame Speech

Thank you Ray. Thank you to the Athletic Wall of Fame Committee of Dick Allegretti, Brian Burke, Dan DeFranza, Dan Fitzpatrick, Augie Genovesi, Mike Hennessy, and Len Sitko for making this possible.

I'm Catholic so I have a lot of relatives. Some of them are here today: my mother; my wife, Gretchen; my son, James; my sister, Mary; and my brother, George.

From just about the day I walked in the door as a freshman at Notre Dame High School, I heard about Rick Gorzynski '63. He was the quarterback, safety, kicker, and punter on the 1961 NDHS football team that was 10-0. He was also a great baseball player.

During my sophomore lunch breaks, Coach Willett explained the option series and the counter play to me. The power sweep was used to entertain the fans and the players. Seven players would come around the end. There was certainly little need to throw a pass.

At the start of my junior year, I failed the football physical because of a hernia. I got in for the last two plays of the last game. I handed off twice.

After the season, I ran laps around Cornell Park in Des Plaines, the city of destiny. When the laps were tiresome, I changed to a five-mile loop through the streets. I ran south on Wolf Road, east on Thacker, north on Pearson, west on Prairie, and north on Wolf Road.

In the spring, I went out for track. Father Devlin, the distance runners' coach, said that I ran like a football player. I took that as a compliment.

For the Conference Meet at Saint Procopius, which is now Benet, I was seeded tenth in the mile. I finished fifth and scored a point.

During the summer before my senior football season, 1966, I threw 200 passes a day and ran five miles a day. At the start of the three-a-day August practices, I won the football players' 600-yard run in 1:21.8.

As a senior, I had the chance to choose my uniform number. I chose number 10 because that was Rick Gorzynski's number.

I was the defensive signal caller, right outside linebacker, and blocking back on the punts. I also got to play some quarterback. In my best game, I had five tackles, three touchdown passes, and one touchdown run in three quarters. When I asked for more playing time, Coach Cole let me run down kickoffs which I was happy to do.

On January 26, 1967, a snowstorm started at 5:00 a.m. There were 23 inches of snow that fell in the next 29 hours. Winds blew at 53 miles per hour. I was working out with the distance runners in the school parking lot that afternoon. Finally, the coach, Father Devlin, said, "All right, you can go in now."

1967 was the first year for the high school two-mile run in the state of Illinois. If I could beat everyone on the team, I'd have the school record. I set the school record three times.

1967 was also the first year for the Notre Dame High School Don Relays. If I could win the mile, I'd have the meet record. I won the mile.

In the District Track Meet, I was seeded 14th in the mile. I won my heat in 4:37.9 to take sixth in the Meet.

The day before the Conference Meet I was elected a co-captain. I was seeded third in the mile. I took second. I was elected most improved runner.

I had the good fortune to be on three championship teams at Notre Dame High School: the 1966 track & field team, the 1966 football team, and the 1967 track & field team.

Thank you to the coaches of those teams: Bill Casey, Jack Cole, Denny Conway, Father Devlin, Al Loboy, Jim Meyer, and Fran Willett.

Thank you to the players of those teams, including the Wall of Famers: Charlie Bilodeau, John Debbout, Bob Feltz, Brian Kelly, Gary Lund, Greg Luzinski, Pete Newell, Mike Newton, Joe Petricca, and Ken Powers.

Notre Dame Miracle I was the new track. Notre Dame Miracle II was the new parking lot. Notre Dame Miracle III took place before Father Stroot's wake at the University of Notre Dame which was named after God's mother. I had dinner with Ray Gorzynski '60 and John Ranos '66 at the University Club. Ray picked up the check.

When my older brothers are busy, I call Ray. Thank you to Ray and John Ranos for nominating me for the Athletic Wall of Fame. This award is very important to me.

I'm on the masters track circuit. Masters means for people over 30. Fortunately for me, my wife is a nurse. I am able to still compete because she takes very good care of me.

I thank God for my family, my coaches, my teachers, my teammates, and my friends. God has been very, very good to me.

RAY GORZYNSKI

In the television show "The Adventures of Ozzie and Harriet," Dave and Rick Nelson had a fraternity brother by the name of Wally Plumpstead who had a big, wonderful laugh. He laughed like Ray Gorzynski. Will Rogers said, *"I never met a man I didn't like until two or more got together on a committee."* Will Rogers never served on a committee with Ray Gorzynski. He was the best.

Ray Gorzynski was the founder of the Notre Dame Alumni Golf Outing. He served on the Notre Dame Dinner Auction Committee. He was the masterful master of ceremonies for the Notre Dame Sports Nights. He distributed premiums at Chicago Bears' home games for the benefit of the Notre Dame Track Fund.

He came to my sons' games. He sat with my sons in the rain at Super Bowl XLI.

Ray did so much to help the school and more than any other Don, he lived the Golden Rule. Here's a Notre Dame cheer from the early 1960s.

Who's a Don
He's a Don
He's a Notre Dame Don
Gorzynski
Gorzynski
Gorzynski

KEN POWERS

Ken Powers was born September 25, 1949 in Chicago. He attended Saint Juliana's School in Edison Park. In the fall of 1963, he was a skinny freshman football player at Notre Dame High School in Niles, Illinois.

Bill Casey was the freshman football coach. One day he told Powers to run laps. Then Casey went inside and forgot about Powers. Powers kept running until after dark when Casey was reminded about him and went out to get him. Powers thought that was normal.

When Powers was a sophomore, he entertained teammates in the cafeteria by talking about his great tackles. He illustrated this with the fingers of one hand walking on a cafeteria table. The fingers of his other hand would be him. He would always make the tackle.

When Notre Dame got new wrestling mats, Powers and some teammates put on a spontaneous impersonation of professional wrestling that was hilarious.

Powers bulked up that winter. He said, "I go home from school and eat. Then I take a nap and get up and eat some more."

In the summer of 1966, he went with my brothers Ned and George and me to the Chicago Bears' training camp at Saint Joseph's College in Rensselaer, Indiana. We worked out together and sought relief in the quarry that was full of water. I was concerned about my brothers. I didn't want them to get too far from Ken and me. So Powers warned them to watch out for Gator Man who would eat them in one bite.

We got good food at training camp. Ken ate it in a unique way. Before he would eat a piece of cake, he said, *"Hi cake. I'm going to eat you."*

Before the first Notre Dame game in 1966, Powers and Mike Shaw were elected co-captains. Powers started at end and inside linebacker. In the game against Saint Francis, he made an interception. In the game against Holy Cross, he caught a 27-yard touchdown pass from Bill Harrington. Powers also blocked a punt, recovered the ball, and ran for another touchdown. For the season, Powers made 85 tackles, leading the team. Notre Dame was 9-0. He was the toughest guy on the team, the nicest and the funniest—a cross between Dick Butkus and Jonathan Winters. He did impersonations from "The Wizard of Oz." He was dedicated and he was funny.

After the season, Powers was voted most valuable player on a team that won every game by an average of 29 points. He also made all-conference and all-state.

In May of 1967, my twin cousins, Kay and Lisa, were in town for my sister Ellen's wedding. Powers went out with Lisa and Pat Hughes escorted Kay. Peggy Phillips and I were the third couple on the triple date.

At graduation at Notre Dame, we received our diplomas in alphabetical order in the school gym. I was sitting in my seat on the gym floor when Powers was walking off the stage. I asked Pete Newell if I should get up and congratulate him. Newell strongly encouraged me to do so. So I did.

Powers started as a 205-pound freshman linebacker at Northeast Missouri State (now Truman State), the alma mater of our high school coach, Fran Willett. He started on the conference champions of 1970 and 1971. He was 220 pounds as a senior and he made honorable mention all-conference.

Powers was in the Phi Sigma Epsilon fraternity and he was treasurer of his senior class. In May, 1972, he graduated with a degree in business administration.

At our 10-year class reunion in the fall of 1977, Coach Casey had put together some film clips from our '66 season. Powers did a great job impersonating the coaches at a team meeting. When an alleged mistake was seen, he hollered, "Who was that? Run that back again." Powers is in the Notre Dame College Prep Athletic Wall of Fame.

From 1983 to 1985, Powers was the Executive Director of the Chamber of Commerce in Mountain Home, Arkansas. Then he moved to Houston and worked in construction sales. I last saw him on the weekend of October 11-12, 1986, when the Bears played the Oilers in Houston. We had dinner together.

On Friday, October 17, 1986, the 1966 team was honored at halftime of the Notre Dame home-coming game. Powers was unable to make it because he wanted to spend any free time with his children. Powers wasn't feeling well and he went to see the doctor. The doctor told Powers that he should go home and make out his will. Nothing could be done. He had an inoperable brain tumor that was cancerous. He didn't make age 40.

Ken Powers died on Friday, August 4, 1989, at his mother's house in Mountain Home. Services were held on Sunday, August 6 at 2:30 p.m. at the Kirby Funeral Home Chapel. He is buried in Kirby's Tucker Memorial Cemetery in Mountain Home. He is sorely missed.

Saint John Vianney Courtyard in Ars

Saint John Vianney

On May 8, 1786, John Vianney was born in Dardilly, France. His Feast Day is August 4. His parents were farmers. When he was 13, he made his First Communion. When he was 20, he was allowed to leave the farm to get an education.

Vianney was raised during the French Revolution when practicing Catholicism was outlawed. Priests were sometimes put to death; Vianney's family hid them.[16] Clandestine Masses were held in barns.

In 1809, he was drafted into the army after he had started to study for the priesthood. Napoleon had come to power and he needed soldiers. Vianney was no soldier. He became ill and was hospitalized as others in his draft were leaving. After his release from the hospital, he was added to another group that was heading out. At the time, the French army was ill-equipped and ceaseless bloodshed eroded morale. Desertion was high.[17] On his way, he went into a church to pray and fell behind again. He ended up in the mountains with a band of deserters where he lived for 14 months. He made the most of his time and opened a school for children.

In March 1810, Vianney resumed his studies after amnesty was granted for deserters. In 1811, he was tonsured—his hair was shaved in preparation for priesthood. In 1812, he went to a minor seminary. In 1813, he went to major seminary where he was considered too slow. Vianney had an especially difficult time learning Latin. Helped by a priest and working with a tutor, he made some progress, but he left the seminary.

Again a priest helped him and appealed to Church authorities. Vianney persevered and his piety made up for his ignorance. In 1814, he received minor orders. In 1815, he was ordained a deacon and then a priest.

In 1818, Vianney was appointed the pastor of Ars. He was great in the confessional. He was there most of the day. Thousands journeyed to Ars to have him hear their confessions. Many suggested that despite his scholastic deficiencies, he had a way of knowing what bothered confessors. It was as if he could read their minds. In Ars, he welcomed the people back to their faith after years of chaos, revolution, and fighting. He was healing wounds—saying Mass and administering the sacraments. In this way, his mission was that of a simple hard-working parish priest nothing more. Yet, his work was powerful and transforming.

On August 4, 1859, he died at the age of 73. At his funeral, the bishop was the celebrant; 300 priests and more than 6,000 people attended.

In 1925, he was canonized as a saint. In 1929, he was named the patron saint of parish priests. Vianney demonstrates the value of the good listener and the passionate presence of a good priest.

Here is the Saint Vianney Prayer:

I love you, O my God, and my only desire is to love You until the last breath of my life. I love You, O my infinitely lovable God, and I would rather die loving You, than live without loving You. I love You, Lord and the only grace I ask is to love You eternally. My God, if my tongue cannot say in every moment that I love You, I want my heart to repeat it to You as often as I draw breath.

On February 21, 2017, a play about his life, "Vianney," was performed at Saint Patrick Church in Lake Forest. Monsignor Dempsey welcomed the audience. Leonardo Defilippis played Saint John Vianney. Leonardo's wife, Patti, of Saint Luke Productions was the director. It was wonderful.

GEORGE HALAS

Quiz—Bears' History

Questions

1. The George Halas Junior Sports Center was built and dedicated in honor of the Bears' Executive and son of founder George "Papa Bear" Halas. At what university is the Center?

2. Early in 1958, Italian singer-songwriter Domenico Modugno recorded a blockbuster mega-hit. At Bears' camp at Saint Joseph's College, defensive back Vic Zucco serenaded the players regularly with what catchy tune that has been covered by dozens of artists—used in movies and commercials to this day?

3. Ed Brown led the Bears as quarterback during much of the 1950s. Ed was featured in ads for Bike Athletic Supporters and what healthy beverage?

4.   Don Kindt played defensive back for the Bears following World War II. While serving during the close of the war, he slept in which famous dictator's bed?
5.   When George Halas was coaching the Bears, what did the players have to do to start off training camp?
6.   Which 1960s Bears' quarterback could find a four leaf clover at the drop of a chin strap prophesying a good day's practice?
7.   The orange "C" was put on the Bears' helmets in 1973. What did it replace?
8.   There are 14 retired Bears' numbers, name as many of these numbers and players as you can.
9.   The Bears have nine championship season as of the start of 2018. Name as many of these as you can.
10.   Name the two Bears' players who have their numbers retired, but are not in the Hall of Fame?

Answers

1.   The George Halas Junior Sports Center is at Loyola University of Chicago. It was dedicated on September 2, 1982.
2.   We know the song as "Volare" and it was also known as Nel blu dipinto di blu ("In the blue that is painted blue"). Dean Martin, David Bowie, Barry White, Paul McCartney, and Vitamin C are just some of the singers who have versions of it.

3. Ed Brown was featured in ads for milk.

4. Don Kindt fought in the Italian campaign. He and many soldiers who had come to take control of Mussolini's villa after the Germans left, took turns sleeping in Benito Mussolini's bed.

5. George Halas had his players run the "Halas Mile" to start things off in training camp.

6. Bill Wade entertained the kids present with this prediction.

7. It replaced the white "C" that had been on the helmets since 1962.

8. The 14 retired Bears' numbers: 3 Bronko Nagurski, 5 George McAfee, 7 George Halas, 28 Willie Galimore, 34 Walter Payton, 40 Gale Sayers, 41 Brian Piccolo, 42 Sid Luckman, 51 Dick Butkus, 61 Bill George, 66 Bulldog Turner, 77 Red Grange, 89 Mike Ditka.

9. The nine Bears' championship seasons: 1921, 1932, 1933, 1940, 1941, 1943, 1946, 1963, 1985.

10. Willie Galimore and Brian Piccolo are not in the Hall of Fame.

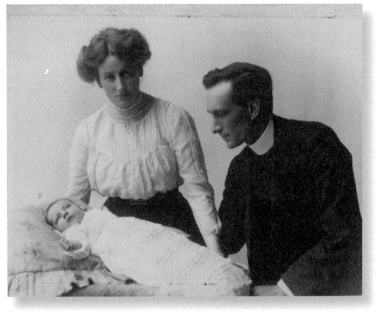

OSWALD CHAMBERS FAMILY

Weddings, Births, and Vacations Should Take Place During the Off-Seasons.

Introduction

Some vocations are demanding. Most Catholic religious orders do not allow members to marry. Depending upon your position with a professional football team, almost everything involving family life is put on hold during the season unless a catastrophe takes place.

Hall of Fame Coach Joe Gibbs is a focused, competitive, and determined man. His staff often spent late nights in the Redskins' offices going over strategies and action steps. There were no clocks in the office (no cell phones at the time either). When Gibbs's wife was in the hospital, he famously bought new clothes for his sons rather than take time to do wash!

Patriots' Head Coach Bill Belichick's habits and his demands are noteworthy as well. From day one of pre-season meetings until the whistle blows on the last game, he expects the full attention of his staff.

My grandfather, George Halas, was playing, coaching, running a team, and helping the NFL to succeed all at the same time. After he retired from playing, his football responsibilities increased with The Depression, World War II, and the various competitive leagues that sprung up. He had to focus. The meaning of this commandment is ***use your time well and focus on what needs to be done***!

TOM BENSON

Tom Benson was a New Orleans native who at only 17 years old enlisted in the Navy in 1945 and served in the Pacific aboard the USS South Dakota. Later, Benson was highly successful in business and built up a chain of automobile dealerships, which led to his ownership of several banks.

In 1985, successful businessman Tom Benson became the owner and Managing General Partner of the New Orleans Saints Football Club. It would be a challenging undertaking. The first two decades saw a small margin of success. And just before the team got much better, disaster struck in 2005 when Hurricane Katrina ravaged the Gulf. The Saints could not play their 2005 season games in their home, the Louisiana Superdome. For a time, the viability of New Orleans as a professional football venue came into question after the economic injury and population decline that resulted.

As New Orleans continued to struggle economically in 2009, the New Orleans Saints finished their season, 13–3, and went on to win the Super Bowl. It was one of the most memorable seasons in NFL history and certainly a boost to the spirit of the city and the region. On the field, Benson's coach, Sean Payton, and his quarterback, Drew Brees, along with many others, have helped establish the Saints as consistent contenders. Saints' fans appreciate the effort.

Off the field, Benson had a positive impact on the community. In fact, many believe he purchased the Saints to keep them home in the "Crescent City." Those who knew him say that the club's charitable involvement has been among his most rewarding endeavors. The Saints' players, coaches, and staff donate their time in volunteer work and charitable outreach. Millions of dollars have been raised by Benson and his team for Saints Hurricane Katrina Fund and Gulf Coast Renewal Fund. The New Orleans Saints partner with local youth-oriented charities to reach as many children as possible. Over 45 foundations and agencies receive monetary donations from the Saints each year. Benson also worked closely with the Ochsner Foundation Hospital in New Orleans with the establishment of the Tom and Gayle Benson Cancer Center, a $20-million treatment complex.

Among many honors, Benson and the Saints received the Good Samaritan Award in Philanthropy. Benson himself was awarded Loyola University of New Orleans' Integritas Vitae Award. He has been inducted into the Sports Faith Hall of Fame.

When I pointed out to Tom Benson that George Halas, Well Mara, Bill Bidwill, and Art Rooney have been inducted into the Sports Faith Hall of Fame, he was concerned. He said, "Most of those guys are dead."

And yet he came to Illinois in February 2012 to be inducted into the Sports Faith Hall of Fame. The only thing he asked was to be inducted first so that he could get back to New Orleans to buy a basketball team.[18] He was accommodated.

It was an honor to be at his wake and funeral in New Orleans March 22-23, 2018.

CHESHIRE ACADEMY

After graduating from Notre Dame of Niles, I enrolled at Cheshire Academy in Connecticut as a post graduate to continue my education. I also wanted to get another year of playing experience on the advice of Coach Joe Yonto. Yonto knew that I aspired to play football for the University of Notre Dame where he worked at the time. Yonto had coached at my alma mater, Notre Dame High School. At Notre Dame University, he was coaching the defensive line for Ara Parseghian. I wanted to play quarterback for the University of Notre Dame.

Coach Yonto also wrote a letter about me to Cheshire's football coach, Steve Kuk. Based on Coach Yonto's letter, Coach Kuk designed a pro-style offense with me passing often for Cheshire.

I was certainly willing to put in the effort to succeed and get into Notre Dame, but serious eye problems scaled back my athletic options the summer before school at Cheshire. Regardless, I enjoyed my experience at Cheshire where I was able to compete in cross country and track. I was a part of the Cheshire Class of 1968.

CHESHIRE IN 1968

The year 1968 was important in many ways. Chris Kita's Valedictorian's Speech was given the day after Robert Kennedy was killed. Two months earlier, Robert Kennedy had turned to Aeschylus after Martin Luther King Junior was assassinated:

"And even in our sleep, pain which cannot forget falls drop by drop upon the heart, until in our own despair, against our will, comes wisdom through the awful grace of God."

Kita said that Dag Hammarskjold, the former Secretary-General of the United Nations, turned to philosophers for answers in troubled times. Kita reminded the class that they would become philosophers themselves.

CHRIS KITA'S VALEDICTORIAN'S SPEECH

"What sort of world is this that we, the Class of 1968, will enter? We will assume a leading role in a society that lacks a norm. What sort of world is this that could allow the events of yesterday to happen? It is written, 'Blessed are the peace-makers, for they shall be called the children of God.' There is only one world in which these things can happen, in which the children of God can be so brutally and senselessly stricken. There is only one world in which murder can become an accepted fact or a political tool, and that is the world we are about to join.

"In 1961 another peacemaker died. He was not assassinated, but his death was no less tragic.[19] Dag Hammarskjold was a man dedicated to peace. He was a man who searched his soul for a key to unlock the illusory balance of principles by which all peoples can live in common peace and brotherhood. He was not satisfied by any key he had discovered, because the key he was searching for was an ideal which can only be approximated. One of the concepts he came across can help lift us out of the muck and mire of our present troubles. It can provide an island of sanity in an insane world. There can be no more fitting tribute to such a man.

"The concept he offers is in his statement: 'For all that has been, thanks; for all that will be, yes.' We owe a great debt to such philosophers, for it is only through thinking that constructive changes can be made, that the key can be discovered. And it is only by this that we can rise above and conquer present tribulations. We can learn something from all the philosophers down through the ages; all that has been said before can help us in our present situation. We are all grateful for the preparation we have received here, preparation which will enable us at least to begin to cope with this world in which we live. We are aware of the development of the philosopher in each of us, a development which should give us a new perspective with which to evaluate this world. We appreciate the attempt to instill in us a set of human values, values which far surpass morals or ethics and provide an ideal to strive for.

"It now remains for us to journey out into this world. And once we enter this world we must assume the burden and responsibility for it. Through our studies we have come to realize the value of the affirmative. We must now utilize this realization. In the face of negative events we must put forth a positive effort to counteract them. The only way we can stop the needless and senseless bloodshed and violence is to strive towards our ideal. Whenever an opportunity to help raise our society from the depths we find it in presents itself, we must all say 'yes.'"

SPEECH FOR LENNY SIMPSON

In 2011, my Cheshire classmate, Lenny Simpson, was inducted into the North Carolina Tennis Hall of Fame. He asked me to write a speech for him. So, I did and included additional instructions. For some reason, he didn't use it. Since I don't want the speech to go to waste, here it is:

(Blow into the microphone.) Is this on? Can you hear me in the back?

The Gettysburg Address was a two and half minute speech. The man who talked before Lincoln talked for two hours and no one remembers what he said.

When I think about being inducted into the North Carolina Tennis Hall of Fame, I remember what Gale Sayers said when the Chicago Bears retired his number, "It's about time."

While I was listening to the other speakers, I remembered what Mark Twain said, "It's a terrible death to be talked to death."

Of all the awards that I have received, this is one of them. It's not the Cheshire Academy Athletic Hall of Fame, but it's something.

There are some people who have said that I don't deserve this induction. I remember what Howard Cosell said, "What these people have said about me is like throwing spitballs at a battleship."

Here are some thoughts from Jackie Vernon.

"My grandfather was an old Indian fighter. My grandmother was an old Indian.

"When I was born, my father spent three weeks trying to find a loophole in my birth certificate."

"This might be hard for you to believe, but I used to be a dull guy. You're probably wondering what changed me from the prosaic deadbeat I was to the effervescent gay blade that I am today." [20]

"Never spit in another man's face unless his moustache is on fire."

Comedian Steven Wright says, *"It's a small world but I wouldn't want to paint it."*

"You can't have everything; where would you put it?"

Henny Youngman used to say, *"Laugh it up folks; these are the jokes. I know you're out there because I can hear you breathing."*

There's no need to kneel. (Then bless the crowd.)

LAWNDALE CHRISTIAN COMMUNITY CHURCH

Three score and seven years ago, my parents brought forth in Evanston, a new baby, conceived in Manhasset, and dedicated to the proposition that all babies are important.

Now we are engaged in the Lawndale Christian Community Church Anniversary, testing whether that baby, or any baby so conceived and so dedicated, can long endure. We are met at Lawndale Christian Community Church. We have come to pray and sing and worship together, in gratitude for my father who dedicated his life that that baby might grow. It is altogether fitting and proper that we should do this.

But in a larger sense, we cannot dedicate—we cannot consecrate—we cannot hallow—this anniversary. The parents, living and dead, who raised me, have consecrated it, far above our poor power to add or detract. The world will little note, nor long remember what we say here, but it can never forget what they did here. It is for us the living, rather, to be dedicated here to the unfinished work which you who listen and pray and sing have thus far so nobly advanced. It is rather for us to be here dedicated to the great task remaining before us—that from the honored dead we take increased devotion to that cause for which he gave the last full measure of devotion—that we here highly resolve that my father shall not have died in vain—that my family, under God, had a new birth on December 1—and that family in the name of The Father, and of The Son, and of The Holy Spirit, shall not perish from the earth.

UNEXPECTED OFF-SEASONS

When I was a junior at Notre Dame High School in Niles, Illinois, I failed the football physical because of a hernia. I found myself in the "off-season." When I was a senior, I was an All-American quarterback and a 4:37 miler. My aspiration to play for the University of Notre Dame ended when my eye doctor, George Jessen, said, *"No more contact sports."* It was "off-season" again, but not for long.

When I got to Cheshire, I saw a notice on a bulletin board for cross-country tryouts. After I had received permission from Doctor Jessen, I went out for cross-country. I won nine races, including the conference championship. Fran Ciak, Glen Cox, Tao Risquez, Vin Pesce, and I finished on the track at halftime of the homecoming football game. I was 14th in the New England Championships and I won a medal.

When I was a student at Cheshire Academy, my hobby was reading. I read an essay that wasn't even assigned. It was "University Days" by James Thurber. Then I read all of the Thurber books that were in the Cheshire Public Library.

I applied to Indiana University, Miami of Ohio, and Ohio State. I was accepted at each of those schools. I was all set to go to Ohio State because that is where James Thurber went.

Over the summer after graduation, Doctor Jessen talked me into going to Indiana University because his son Mike had gone there. I went there sight unseen. I was an English major because I wanted to be a writer. I really majored in James

Thurber and E. B. White. I read their books and the articles about them in the wonderful Indiana University Library.

I worked on my first book for 40 years before I got it published. I have had six books published.

AUNT BETTY McCASKEY

My aunt Betty McCaskey liked the Chicago Bears, Frank Sinatra, and Tony Bennett. On Saturday, May 27, 1967, my aunt was at my sister Ellen's wedding in Illinois. I attended the wedding, but I didn't go to the reception because I had a track meet. It was the conference meet and I was a co-captain.

After the meet, Aunt Betty was one of the few people who was interested in how I did. I was seeded third in the mile run and I took second. We won the meet by 29 points. Aunt Betty said to me, "I've been to enough track meets to know that second place in the conference mile is quite an accomplishment."

On Saturday, June 14, 1980, I ran the 5 miles in the Red Roses Run in Lancaster, Pennsylvania. My time was 31:36.

Right before I went to bed the night before the race, my uncle, Tom McCaskey, said to me, *"If you have to get up in the middle of the night, don't fall down the stairs because you'll wake me."*

In the middle of the night, Aunt Betty fell down the stairs and woke Uncle Tom and me. An ambulance came to the house and took care of her. Aunt Betty apologized profusely to me because she felt that she had disturbed my pre-race rest. She was so thoughtful she would probably apologize that her funeral took place during the Chicago Bears' veteran minicamp.

OSWALD CHAMBERS

Oswald Chambers was born on July 24, 1874, in Aberdeen, Scotland. He was a missionary to Egypt during World War I. From David McCasland's biography, *Abandoned to God*, we know that Chambers had to learn to soften his style of preaching, but not his content. He did not water down the Bible. He also learned not to defend himself. His faith helped him to keep silent. He felt that God would defend him.

Chambers also believed that prayer helped him to get in step with God. Prayer wasn't for God to bless his plans. Prayer was work and battle, asking and receiving.

Christ died for Chambers so he felt obliged to do something for Him. Chambers felt that the world was his parish. Chambers and his wife felt called to serve God and then each other. He did not hold anything back. He never despaired of anyone because of the way God changed him. He let mistakes correct themselves and he did not criticize. He was a deep person because he drew his strength from God.

Chambers read many other books besides the Bible. He enjoyed classical music and nature. He wrote poetry and newspaper articles. He was graceful and unhurried. He sought the company of children.

Before his sermons, he had quiet time to prepare himself. He was 35 when he married his wife, Gertrude ("Biddy), who was almost 26. His approach to the future was, *"Trust God and do the next thing."*

Chambers was consistent in how he lived and in what he said. He trusted God patiently. When someone was doing something wrong, Chambers prayed for God to convict him.

Chambers urged his congregations to give up their rights to themselves to God and do His will. When we follow God's will, we will be joyful and blessed. Once, when Chambers was on a ship, he had difficulty finding a place to pray. Then he crawled into a lifeboat for some time with God.

Chambers had a great sense of humor which he used to plow the land. Then he planted the seeds of faith. He even asked for God's blessing on a boxing match. Instead of relying on common sense, he waited for God to fulfill His purpose. He trusted God every day.

Chambers and his wife never discussed money matters in front of other people. He died on November 15, 1917, in Cairo, Egypt from appendicitis at the age of 43. Biddy's mission, after he died, was not to sell books, but to help people. She wrote books from his sermons which she had taken down shorthand. The daily devotional, *My Utmost for His Highest*, has this entry for October 12th: *"The worth of a man is revealed in his attitude to ordinary things when he is not before the footlights."*

During World War II, 40,000 copies of Chambers' books were burned in the London Blitz. His wife calmly waited on the Lord for an answer. Now millions of people all around the world read his devotional every day.

NEHEMIAH

In the 5th century B.C., Nehemiah rebuilt the walls of Jerusalem. It didn't happen all at once, but it happened.

His prayer is in Nehemiah 1:5-11. The challenge to our own prayer lives is that sometimes it's okay to use run-on sentences.

After Nehemiah had arrived in Jerusalem, he rested for three days. Then he said, *"Come let us rebuild."* Others caught the vision. Still others mocked the re-builders. Nehemiah was prepared for the mockers. He responded in a gentlemanly manner.

Prayer is an excellent preparation. We should pray before we go to the person in authority, the people who help you, and the people who will mock you.

Nehemiah had three important steps in his prayers. First, he praised God. Then Nehemiah confessed his sins. Finally, he made his requests.

Nehemiah also analyzed the situation. He inspired others to join the project. He knew that God would provide the necessary strength. He also knew that his opposition wouldn't disappear. To set a good example for his people, he did not profit from the rebuilding of the wall.

Nehemiah received four messages from his opponents for a meeting. He refused to meet with them. He received a fifth message from one of his opponents for a meeting. Nehemiah refused this meeting, too. He also denied the rumors of his desire for kingship. He was told to flee, but he refused.

It took 52 days to finish the wall.

Nehemiah's people fasted. They wore sackcloth. They covered their heads with dust. They confessed their sins. They read from the book of the law of the Lord. The book was their blueprint for religious living.

Nehemiah wanted to increase the population of Jerusalem. Perhaps he wanted to make sure there would be enough participation. The walls could have been paid for through fundraisers.

Let us be joyous people. Let us be happy in the Lord. The Ammonites and the Moabites were enemies of Nehemiah's people. In our own day, those who resemble them are denigrators and second-guessers.

When Nehemiah made his final prayers, he mentioned his good works, but he relied on God's mercy. Nehemiah's people who married outside the faith had children who had trouble with the language. A similar problem exists today. There are some students who do not study Greek or Latin.

My favorite verse from Nehemiah is 2:18: *"Let us be up and building, and they undertook the good work with vigor."*

Other Bible verses are also helpful. Proverbs 3:5-6, *"Trust in the Lord with all your heart, on your own understanding rely not; in all your ways be mindful of him, and he will make straight your paths."*

Psalm 37:4-5, *"Take delight in the Lord, and he will grant you your heart's requests. Commit to the Lord your way; trust in him, and he will act."*

Ephesians 6:10, *"Draw your strength from the Lord and from His mighty power."*

SAINT JOAN OF ARC

SAINT JOAN OF ARC

One of the most celebrated saints is Saint Joan of Arc (Jeanne la Pucelle) who has been featured in movies, plays, books, and art. The Maid, as she is called, was born on the Epiphany, January 6, 1412, in Domremy in Northeastern France. Her family was of modest means. Her mother taught her household skills, but Joan did not learn to read and write.[21] Joan loved to go to church and pray. She lived during the Hundred Years War when England had taken hold of much of France and various other territories in France were aligned with the English. Occasionally, danger crept into town from the ongoing conflict. Stories of the suffering would often make their way to Joan's family by people passing through the village.

Joan heard voices at a young age. Saints Michael the Archangel, Catherine of Alexandria, and Margaret of Antioch (all found in the local church's stained glass windows) spoke to her, telling the young teenager that God wanted her to drive the English out of France and bring the Dauphin (the uncrowned Charles VII) to Reims for his coronation.[22] To begin her mission, she traveled to Vaucouleurs to see an official who might lead her to the King. It took two trips to gain the credibility she needed. On the second trip, she predicted French success at the Battle of Rouvray near Orléans, which occurred. This opened the door for her to visit the French Royal Court.[23]

All throughout her adventures, Joan was met with skepticism. Those around King Charles VII were cautious about giving her support, which they believed might lead to charges of the French royal being assisted by a witch. After some research and weeks of interviews by theologians, Joan was deemed a virtuous girl, but the King seemed irresolute throughout. In truth, Joan was a strange ally for the king to have beside him.

At last, Joan was allowed to lead a French force at Orleans. Joan's presence changed the stakes of the war; suddenly what had been a conflict over succession to the French throne became a religious war. In battle, Joan would carry a religious themed banner that included the words "Jesus, Mary," and the figure of God the Father with two kneeling angels presenting the fleur-de-lis.[24] With Joan clothed in white, the French soldiers fought with renewed vigor. More victories occurred and eventually Charles VII was crowned King in Reims in 1429.

Joan of Arc would be wounded twice in battle. She was always working to motivate the King and the army leaders to take more decisive action—after all, God was on the King's side!

Joan of Arc continued to lead efforts to drive the English out, but the war would continue for some time after Joan's involvement. Joan was captured near Compiegne outside the gates of the town. Her captors, were the Burgundians, at that time, independent and involved in disputes with the French. Joan was sold to the English for a high price. A period of incarceration took place and a trial for heresy and witchcraft insured a final solution for her enemies. Illiterate and unsophisticated, Joan had no representation at trial and no real support. Brave beyond her years throughout the whole ordeal, at last the court, run by Religious and backed by the English, elicited an admittance of guilt.

Joan of Arc dressed in men's clothes at times to hide from the English when traveling. She also dressed like a man on campaigns and in prison to avoid any sexual attacks. Her accusers said this was evidence of witchcraft. A group of educated Religious scholars with preconceived notions of her guilt, who had been hurt by her success, contributed to her trial. Other stories suggests that some Religious were forced to take part in the trial due to threats.

Joan's confession came after she was sentenced to burning at the stake and she was frightened before a large crowd. Afterwards, promises made to her were not kept. She was to be free to go to Mass and receive Communion. Her captors were also to free her from her chains, which had been an almost constant companion. When these promises were broken, Joan regained her courage and recanted her confession. She was sentenced to death. On May 30, 1431, Joan was burned at the stake in Rouen. To insure no credible relics could be saved, her ashes were thrown into the Seine.

Twenty-five years after the trial, the Pope ordered a rehearing of the case and she was rehabilitated as a true and faithful daughter of the Church. The collection of material from her trials was especially helpful in gathering information on this great saint. Saint Joan of Arc was canonized in 1920. She is the patron saint of France. May 30 is her feast day.

SHAKESPEARE

Quiz—Anything Goes

Questions

1. Can you name three 1st-round draft choices in Chicago who have the first name Kyle?
2. When Don Rickles came into the bedroom on his wedding night with an Olympic torch what did he say?
3. What did William Shakespeare's father say to William Shakespeare?
4. Martin Luther King Junior played quarterback for Morehouse College–True or false?
5. His team was constantly penalized for delay of game because he kept making speeches in the huddle–True or false?
6. What was Billy Graham's favorite Commandment?
7. Johnny Carson once asked Ed McMahon, "What's it like to be half Catholic and half Jewish?"
8. What did Melvil Dewey invent?
9. Before there was marketing, water was known as saliva supplement–True or false?
10. Mark Twain said, "Adam and Eve had many advantages, but the principal one was that they escaped___(what)?

Answers

1. Kyle Fuller, Kyle Long, and Kyle Schwarber
2. Don Rickles said: "Let the games begin."
3. William Shakespeare's father said: Make plays.
4. Martin Luther King Junior did play quarterback for Morehouse College–True.
5. MLK's team was not constantly penalized for delay of game because he kept making speeches in the huddle–False.
6. Billy Graham's favorite Commandment was: Honor your father and your mother. He and his wife had five children.
7. Ed McMahon replied: "You still have to go to Confession, but at least you can bring your lawyer."
8. Melvil Dewey invented the Dewey Decimal System.
9. Water was not known as saliva supplement–False.
10. From *Pudd'nhead Wilson*, "teething"

GEORGE HALAS RECEIVES SWORD OF LOYOLA

REMEMBER THE HUPMOBILE AND THE ORIGINAL MEETING.

INTRODUCTION

The Hupmobile showroom in Canton, Ohio, was the site of the original membership meeting of what would become the National Football League. George Halas and the other founders sat on running boards and bumpers. They planned the league and got together at least once a year to make adjustments and rule on items of concern. For decades, professional football was at best a humble enterprise. In fact, only two teams survived from the start, the Bears and Cardinals.[25]

The first half of NFL history, up until about the first Super Bowl, was lean and mean. Some fans like to confine their thoughts to the modern era as defined by the start of the Super Bowl, but that excludes about 50 years of football history.

One way or another, there was a league champion from the earliest days. Early on, the owners looked at the records and declared the champion at their annual meeting. It was complicated because team schedules were radically different—some played a few games a year, others played many. But it didn't take long to fix the scheduling and create the championship game to decide the best in the league.

Like the Dead Ball Era in baseball, the early NFL history is fascinating from many different perspectives. There was a time when the NFL players were paid by the game. At one time in Green Bay, there were no locker rooms and players got dressed before arriving at the field. Sometimes in icy weather, a team would round up gym shoes before a game to replace football cleats—better traction won more than one big game!

Many young fans might want to look back at Paul Brown—a coach who was as serious as Bill Belichick and as professorial as Bill Walsh. Brown introduced classrooms, planned practices like military exercises, valued talent over color preference, and recruited intelligent players.

Before science and research went into player selection, a scrawny Pittsburgh kid got barely a look at Steelers' camp before he was released. He appealed to the Cleveland Browns Head Coach Paul Brown for a tryout and he was told to come back for next year's camp. Colts Head Coach Weeb Ewbank didn't wait and was the man who saw potential in Johnny Unitas and signed him.

After Ewbank moved to the Jets, he saw potential in a kid whose family had worked the mills in Beaver Falls who had suffered knee injuries at Alabama—Joe Namath. Both quarterbacks led their teams to championships.

George Halas played against Olympian Jim Thorpe and signed the first "lights out" talent of the game in Red Grange. Halas was a Rose Bowl MVP and he had a go at baseball with the New York Yankees. Later, many players, including Halas, donned their country's uniform to serve the United States during war.

Remembering the Hupmobile is more than an old corny battle cry of the NFL; it's an invitation for fans to look back at the remarkable history of the game and its players, both saints and sinners, but most of all flesh and blood Americans who often did the best they could with the gifts God gave them.

The meaning of this commandment is *live with passion, inspired by those good people who came before you.*

George Halas and the Chicago Bears' Winning Ways

In the summer of 1915, my grandfather, George Halas, worked for Western Electric in Chicago. On Saturday, July 24, the company was scheduled for a ride on a ship called the Eastland in the Chicago River. My grandfather missed the boat; it rolled over on its side and 844 people died. If he hadn't missed the boat, the National Football League, the Chicago Bears, and I might not be here. Sometimes it's okay to be late.

My grandfather lettered in football, basketball, and baseball at the University of Illinois. He graduated with a degree in engineering in 1918. After my grandfather had graduated from college, he was in the service at the Great Lakes Naval Station. He played sports for them, too. He was the most valuable player in the 1919 Rose Bowl. You could look it up! He played right field for the 1919 New York Yankees and batted .091. Then he played for the 1919 Hammond Pros football team.

On March 18, 1920, George Chamberlain met with my grandfather in Chicago. Chamberlain was the general superintendent of the Staley Company in Decatur. Halas was working in the bridge department of the Chicago, Burlington, & Quincy Railroad.

Chamberlain offered Halas the opportunity to learn the starch business and be the company's athletic director and football coach. He could also play on the Staley football and baseball teams. Halas accepted. The sports headline in the March 19, 1920, *Decatur Review* read "George 'Chic' Hallas Joins Staley Forces."

In 1921, there was a recession. Mister Staley couldn't afford to finance the football team anymore. He gave my grandfather $5,000 worth of advertising to move the team to Chicago with the stipulation that the team nickname be the Staleys for 1 year. So, in 1921, the team was the Chicago Staleys; they won the first of nine championships.

In the winter of 1922, the team name was changed to the Chicago Bears and it's been that way ever since. On February 18, my grandfather and my grandmother, Min, got married. Grandchildren of Mister Staley sometimes wonder what their lives would have been like if their grandfather had sold the company and kept the team.[26]

My grandfather was an optimist. America needed optimists as it battled through The Depression and two world wars during the 20th century. Those who knew my grandfather would tell you that he lived life with a passion every day and seldom looked back. His focus was always on football and he had a gift for providing support and encouragement.

You will find Halas quotes spread out in books and on the internet. Here are some of my favorites along with my thoughts on them.[27]

"Don't do anything in practice that you wouldn't do in the game."

Halas came from a family that believed in hard work. He had no interest in wasting time because he believed there was no time for it. If you were wasting time, you were taking away time that you needed to apply elsewhere. And when he brought his team together, he wanted no wasted motions. When you waste time in practice, you waste it for everyone present.

"Find out what the other team wants to do. Then take it away from them."

In competition of any kind, an opponent sets out to defeat you. And according to Halas, the best way to defeat competition is to stop them from doing what they want. If your opposition likes to run, you stop their running game. If they like to pass, you stop their passing game. If they win by taking advantage of your mistakes, don't make mistakes.

"Many people flounder about in life because they do not have a purpose, an objective towards which to work."

A good coach likes to stick with a game plan, but the best coaches like to win. The best coaches have goals and they move forward from there. When Halas started out as the manager and coach of the Staleys, his objective was to build the best team. When the Staleys were turned over to Halas, his objective was to make the Staleys a success financially and on the field. When Halas found himself at the center of a new professional football league, his objective was to make the new league a success. He was building a team, developing a winning program, and establishing a viable league—all at once.

Halas was fierce after a loss—his wrath was legendary, but it lasted for a short time. Regardless of a game's outcome, Halas put it behind him and started thinking about next week's opponent.

"If you live long enough, lots of nice things happen."

George Halas took good care of himself in terms of diet and exercise. Good goals and hard work led to success, but he also believed it was important to live long to see the success! Like many former football players, Halas had his share of wounds, some of which would dog him for the rest of his life, but he set out to do his best to maintain his health in ways that he could. While much of the world was still thinking retirement at age 65, Halas was coaching into his 70s and he managed the club well into his 80s.

"Nobody who ever gave his best regretted it."

In sports, it is common knowledge that the best teams are highly principled and the best coaches are hard to please. Great effort makes the most sense after the performance, after the win. Regret comes with falling short, but satisfaction comes with optimum effort.

"Nothing is work unless you'd rather be doing something else."

The most satisfying efforts are those that we take on without regret. The hungry athlete takes on exercise, study, training, and repetition with satisfaction knowing that it is leading to goals and objectives. If an athlete no longer shares his or her team's goals and aspirations, training becomes work. The athlete must overcome his opponents, but the most difficult thing to overcome is one's own misgivings. At some point in an athlete's career, it is time to move on.

"Never go to bed a loser."

We have all heard that to have a good marriage we should never go to bed angry. We should never leave any unresolved issues haunting us at night if possible. Halas took this advice a step further. We should never go to bed without having done what we can to make our lives successful and feeling like a success. We all lose at times, but a loser is someone with a damaged ego, who believes himself or herself to be a loser. Halas would say that you should never accept those kinds of self-doubts. Do your best and believe that you are a winner and you will be one.

HALAS'S CONTRIBUTIONS TO THE GAME OF FOOTBALL

George Halas coached for 40 seasons and accumulated 324 wins, 151 losses, and 31 ties. The Bears won six NFL Championships with Halas as coach and a total of eight as NFL owner.[28] He was enshrined in Pro Football Hall of Fame's charter class of 17 members on September 7, 1963. Halas was named AP Coach of the Year, the Sporting News Coach of the Year, and the UPI NFL Coach of the Year for the 1963 and the 1965 seasons.

If anyone could be called the Father of the NFL, it would be George Halas. In this way, his nickname, Papa Bear says it all. He loved the fans and was dedicated to his friends, family, and faith. Halas and a small group of men developed the framework for professional football in the most humble circumstances—a meeting in a car showroom in Canton, Ohio. It took decades to make it work. No one worked as hard or as long as Halas.

Halas never really retired from football. Any awards and honors that came his way would take place during his "career." When he received the Sword of Loyola at the Conrad Hilton, he said:

Sixty years ago I offered my heart and my helmet to the Lord. My heart is still beating and my helmet still fits. I pray the Divine Coach finds me worthy to be on His first team.

Halas drove hundreds of men to make them the best players they could be. At times he could be ruthless in his pursuit of excellence, but he was always relentless in his abiding love of his team. Books are full of stories on how tough he could be. As a player, Halas broke his jaw and his leg, he twisted ankles and knees, and bruised and broke ribs. He led his teams as a players' coach and although he was tough and disciplined, he always treated his players as men.

In the early annals of the Bears, Halas had attracted the toughest of players. Even the name Bears conjures up an impression of physical abandonment that is in large part his making along with people like George Trafton, Bronko Nagurski, Doug Atkins, Ed Sprinkle, Dick Butkus, Mike Ditka, Mike Singletary, Brian Urlacher, and many others.

Halas is a larger-than-life figure for many sports fans. Although his life was hard, it was fantastic on so many levels. His life story is a living history of 20th Century America. Stamped upon his character were lessons from The Great Depression, World War I, and World War II. In so many ways, his life was successful because he had faith, worked hard, and never gave up. He saw problems as opportunities. He moved on from setbacks at lightning speed.

It is customary for sportswriters to devote a chapter in their autobiographies that includes their own personal list of top athletes, coaches, teams, etc. In Warren Brown's book named after his long running Chicago American column, *Win, Lose, or Draw*, he wrote:

In the professional field George Halas and the Chicago Bears year in and year out, will do for me. I am not too hard to please as long as I have the best, doing anything.[29]

MY RESPONSIBILITIES

As one out of many Bears' inheritors, I have prayerfully considered the future of the team. Here is what I have discerned.[30]

George Halas was my grandfather and that's a great legacy. I work for the Bears and that's a great opportunity. I have it made because Christ died for my sins which we don't have time to discuss right now.

I believe that God has a plan for everyone and for every family. We have the freedom to be obedient. I think that God's plan for me is to work for the Bears. I choose to be obedient.

God gave me faith, a wonderful family, and a great legacy. As a mature Boy Scout, I feel prepared.

I hope that we never sell the team even though that would give us a lot of money. Satan offered Jesus all the kingdoms of the world. The Waltons never sold Waltons' Mountain.

From Robert Pinsky's essay, "Responsibilities of the Poet," we know this. *"So one great task we have to answer for*

is the keeping of an art that we did not invent, but were given,
so that others who come after us can have it if they want it, as
free to choose it and change it as we have been."

The same responsibility applies to our Bears' legacy.
With God's faith, I try to be obedient to His plan for my life.
With God's hope, I try to be a voice of encouragement. With
God's love, I try to exemplify Jesus.

Aunt Kay Adelman

My father's fondest memory of his father Dick McCaskey was
when the doctors gave up on our Kay at Saint Joseph's Hospital. My father said:

"She was suffering from erysipelas and was so thin you could
see through her. Dick refused to accept the doctors' verdict
and their despair. [31] *He took me with him to Saint Joseph's. He*
cajoled her into eating creamed spinach. He really saved her
life. She was so thin that we named her Spook."

My father was grateful to his sister, Kay, because of her
research on family history. Thanks to her, we know that the
McCaskey house in Lancaster came down in 1937 or 1938,
when my father was nineteen.

In the spring of 1968, I visited Aunt Kay in Norfolk, Virginia. We walked along the beach for a long time. Finally, she
said, *"We can walk from here to Florida if you like. Or we can*
turn around and go back." We went back.

On Saturday, May 25, 1985, my wife, Gretchen, and I visited
Aunt Betty, Aunt Julie, Aunt Kay, Aunt Maggie, Uncle Jim, and

Cousin Lisa in Hummelstown, Pennsylvania. Aunt Kay made a superb lunch for everyone. She worked so hard that I asked her if she remembered the Biblical story of Martha and Mary. I reminded her, *"I'll only be with you a short while."*

On Monday, March 26, 2001, Aunt Kay arranged for my wife and my children and I to have a tour of McCaskey High School. She also gave me a McCaskey High School necktie.

Kay was our Katherine the Great.

Lately she was slow out of the gate.

Kind forever, ceasing never

She did not hesitate.

Mike Ditka at Tight End

Bears' history comes with a lot of Mike Ditka. Six years at tight end (1961-1966) and 11 years (1982-1992) as head coach. During his time with the team, the Bears won 2 NFL Championships. He was a big part of both.

Ditka's time as the coach or "da coach" tends to overshadow his playing days, but he was a special tight end. "Iron Mike" came from Aliquippa High School and the University of Pittsburgh. When he came to the Bears, he could block like an offensive lineman and catch like a wide receiver. He could also run like a fullback.

Ditka's 75 pass receptions in 1964 set a record that was not eclipsed until 1980 after the NFL season had been extended to 16 games![32] For his 6 years on the Bears as a player, Ditka had 316 receptions for 4,503 yards and 34 touchdowns. Ditka was the first tight end elected to the Pro Football Hall of Fame.

CHILDHOOD FOOTBALL GAMES

When it came to football, we were like children who receive a parlor game for Christmas. Our motto was, "Let's get started; we can learn the rules later."

After the games, older brothers quizzed younger ones on the fundamentals.

"How many points for a touchdown?"
"Six."
"How many points for a field goal?"
"Three."
"How many points for a safety?"
"Two."
"How many points for a point after a touchdown?"
"One."
"How many points for a point after a field goal?"
"One."
"Wrong. There is no such thing as a point after a field goal."
"Check."

As football players, we recognized our responsibility to the community that supported our games. We participated in many civic functions. We were Cub Scouts and then Boy Scouts. We were altar boys and then patrol boys.

All of us were raised with discipline and love and each of us was a special case.

J.C. CAROLINE

On January 17, 1933, J.C. Caroline was born in Warrenton, Georgia. He was named after his father, James Caroline. When he was a boy, he was given the initials J.C. for a nickname. The nickname stuck for the rest of his life. He went to Booker T. Washington High School in Columbia, South Carolina. Buddy Young recruited him to play football for the University of Illinois.[33]

In 1953, J.C. was a sophomore running back who made All-American and led the nation in rushing. In 1955, he played for the Toronto Argonauts and the Montreal Alouettes in the Canadian Football League. Then he earned a physical education degree from Florida A&M University.

In 1956, J.C. was a 7th round choice of the Bears in the NFL Draft. He played running back, defensive back, and special teams for the Bears from 1956 through 1965. He played in the 1957 Pro Bowl. He played on the Bears' 1963 Championship team.

On November 17, 1963, the Bears played the Green Bay Packers at Wrigley Field. J.C. made a great tackle on a kickoff. The Bears won 26–7. In the film session the next week, the team gave J.C. a great round of applause.

After his playing career, J.C. was an assistant coach and a recruiter for the University of Illinois. Then he taught physical education at Urbana Junior High School. In 1980, he was inducted into the College Football Hall of Fame.

When J.C. played for Illinois, Charlie Finn was the team manager. Many years later, Charlie asked J.C. to preach where Charlie went to church. J.C. delivered two wonderful sermons: one for the adults and one for the children.

On Saturday, November 25, 2017, at 12:00 p.m., the Stone Creek Church in Urbana celebrated the life of J.C. who had died on November 17. The Reverend B.J. Tatum officiated. Pastor Tatum told us that J.C.'s daughter Jolynn said he had died peacefully. J.C. was prepared for the inevitable. He tried to get everyone to heaven that he could. He knew his Lord. He had support from his family. He left peacefully. J.C. was an excellent husband, father, grandfather, and great grandfather.

SAINT BLAISE

Saint Blaise

Athletes are reminded of how our lives are in someone else's hands—any day on the field may be the last. Many players thank God for their talents and pray regularly. Catholics and many other Christians often look to the saints for intercession. Saint Blaise is one of the **Fourteen Holy Helpers**, a group of saints venerated for their effective intercession against various diseases.[34]

He is the patron saint of wool combers and sufferers from throat diseases.

The first known record of the saint's life comes from the medical writings of Aëtius Amidenus who lived after Saint Blaise and likely wrote about Blaise in the late 5th or early 6th century.[35] Amidenus depicts Blaise helping patients suffering from objects stuck in their throats. Blaise is said to have performed a cure of a boy who had a fishbone in his throat who was choking. Among other healing miracles credited to Blaise, he was said to cure diseased beasts during his refuge in the country away from persecution that had come to pass under Emperor Diocletian beginning in 303. Diocletian demanded that Christians comply with traditional Roman religious practices. In 316, the governor of Cappadocia and of Lesser Armenia, Agricola, had Bishop Blaise arrested for being a Christian. Saint Blaise was tortured with iron combs, beaten, and beheaded.

On February 3, Saint Blaise's feast day, crossed candles are placed against the throat and the priest, deacon, or lay minister says:

"Through the intercession of Saint Blaise, bishop and martyr, may God deliver you from all ailments of the throat and from every other evil: in the name of the Father, and of the Son and of the Holy Spirit. Amen."

Like other sacramentals, the Blessing of the Throats encourages good thoughts and devotion.

HOLY HELPERS

Fourteen Holy Helpers Prayer

A popular prayer of 14 angels based on the 14 Holy Helpers was used in the opera Hansel and Gretel by Engelbert Humperdinck:

> When at night I go to sleep,
> Fourteen angels watch do keep,
> Two my head are guarding,
> Two my feet are guiding;
> Two upon my right hand,
> Two upon my left hand.
> Two who warmly cover
> Two who o'er me hover,
> Two to whom 'tis given
> To guide my steps to heaven.
> Sleeping softly, then it seems
> Heaven enters in my dreams;
> Angels hover round me,
> Whisp'ring they have found me;
> Two are sweetly singing,
> Two are garlands bringing,
> Strewing me with roses
> As my soul reposes.
> God will not forsake me
> When dawn at last will wake me.

GUY CHAMBERLIN

Quiz—Bears' Players

Questions

1. Which Bear defensive end went to college on a basketball scholarship; was a high jumper; and hurdled blockers?

2. Which popular Chicago sports anchor and slim Bears' receiver put five-pound weights in his armpits for the team weigh-ins so the coaches wouldn't cut him for being too light?

3. Which 1985 Bear defensive lineman didn't play football until 11th grade? What was he doing prior to that?

4. Which Bears running back had a great sense of humor and was the best on the team at throwing rolled up socks in the locker room after practice?

5. Which Bears player from the earliest days of the Decatur Staleys/Bears went on to become one of the top 10 head coaches of all time based on championships won.

6. What Columbia University quarterback signed up with the Bears to lead the awesome "modified" T Formation to greatness?

7. Who was "Mr. Clean, the hitman" according to the Super Bowl Shuffle.

8. Former Bears' Defensive Coordinator Buddy Ryan named the "46 defense" after which player's number.

9. Brian Urlacher was the most recent Bears' player elected into the Pro Football Hall of Fame. Which player who played most of his career for the Bears preceded Brian in his election (and induction)?

10. In 1968 which Bears' player, who had led the nation in rushing in 1964 at Wake Forest, took over for an injured Gale Sayers.

Answers

1. Doug Atkins was a leaper.
2. Johnny Morris was a slight man, but an excellent player and huge Chicago TV personality.
3. Dan Hampton was playing in his high school marching band before he finally played football.
4. Walter Payton had a Hall of Fame sense of humor.
5. Guy Chamberlin played for George Halas and then coached against him on his way to winning 4 NFL Championships as a player/coach.
6. Sid Luckman had all the right skills for a new version of the T Formation that was much more complex than the previous one.
7. Gary Fencik was great on the field and great in the Super Bowl Shuffle.
8. Doug Plank was number 46.
9. Richard Dent got the nod before Urlacher.
10. Brian Piccolo filled in for Sayers before Piccolo's illness.

FATHER BURKE MASTERS AND JOE MADDON

ALL PREVIOUS GAMES ARE PREPARATION FOR THE NEXT ONE.

INTRODUCTION

At the end of the day when you have given it all you have and you have come up short, don't be discouraged. Everything you do today prepares you for tomorrow. And the future holds great promise.

Pittsburgh Steelers' Head Coach Chuck Noll was said to be a tomorrow kind of guy—always looking ahead. Steelers' owner, Art Rooney, had great optimism for what was ahead and he had great patience with his team. My grandfather preached the principle of looking ahead with promise to everyone around the Bears. Sure he got upset and was disappointed when the Bears lost, but he always shook it off and a little later he would bounce back and say: "Who do we play next week."

Bill Belichick has high standards and expects much from his players and coaches. He commands everyone to just "do your job." But it seems like minutes after every season, he is thinking ahead—what do the Patriots need to do?

If you watch the great coaches during a game, you can see the intensity; sometimes it's demonstrable, sometimes it is a quiet kind of burn, but they are certainly in the moment. Halas would roam up and down the sidelines and manage his team like it was part of him. His strong hands would latch onto the back of a player's jersey and he would thrust the player into the game—like an extension of his arm. It was all real, all now and all personal. But when it was done, it was finished— *"Who do we play next week."*

The meaning of this commandment is **look ahead with hope and confidence**.

10 COACHING PRINCIPLES FROM THE NFL

My grandfather, George Halas, was one of the founders of what is now the National Football League. He played professional football himself for 10 years and coached for 40. My mother had 11 children, enough to field our own team. Today, she is 95, yet very much involved in the management of one of the greatest sports enterprises, the Chicago Bears. My family included educators, musicians, and military men. Growing up in the McCaskey-Halas family, we got plenty of coaching.

Here are five personal principles culled from NFL legends that coaches/trainers should help instill in their "players."[36]

Never go to bed a loser.—George Papa Bear Halas

My grandfather succeeded in a fledging professional football business through The Great Depression and World War II. His Chicago Bears became a premier sports enterprise and this little principle was his way to promote exercise, effort, and fortitude every day. He willed everyone around him to give their best effort every day so they could sleep well knowing they had done everything possible.

Treat everyone with kindness, but never let anyone mistake kindness for weakness.—Art Rooney, Senior.

Rooney was another early NFL pioneer and like Halas, he was no wilting lily. A boxer, a talented baseball player, and a sports promoter—Rooney established the Pittsburgh Steelers and led a remarkable family that continues to wrap itself around sports, entertainment, and great causes.

Love and respect all, but fear no one.—*Wellington Mara*

Wellington Mara built the New York Giants football team, which was founded by his father Tim, a legal bookmaker. Mara took a personal interest in his players' needs and he was one of the most advanced thinking owners and a remarkable team-player negotiator.

You don't necessarily have to like your players, but as a leader you must love them.—*Vince Lombardi*

Lombardi graduated magna cum laude from Fordham in 1937 and taught high school for 12 years. In the NFL, he was a legendary motivator who focused on basics and preparation. He had an expanded idea of love: *"Love is loyalty, love is teamwork, love respects the dignity of the individual. This is the strength of any organization."*

Focus on your job—focus on what you and do it right.—*Bill Belichick*

Bill Belichick is not just one of the most successful coaches in NFL history, he is one of the most hard-nosed. He runs the tightest of organizations. Belichick's organization focuses on personal responsibility that leads to organization excellence. He can often be heard in key situations telling a player, "just do your job."

The great NFL coaches would tell us to make each day count, respect and treat others with kindness without being taken advantage of, value the dignity of others, and focus on getting the job done.

Here are five NFL principles for coaches/trainers that should help improve any team.

"Don't do anything in practice that you wouldn't do in the game."—George Halas.

Plan and prepare for what you need to accomplish. Focus on what you need to do every day. Maintain your focus on team objectives. If your team is wasting time, that's a lot of time to waste and takes away opportunity and energy that needs to be productive. Winning teams use time wisely.

Regardless of what happens, a team controls its attitude, approach, and response.—Tony Dungy

Tony Dungy retired after 28 years of coaching and a Super Bowl XLI Championship with the Indianapolis Colts. Dungy currently serves as a sports analyst for NBC's Sunday Night Football. He is also a bestselling author who writes about football, faith, and life. Dungy's principle states that a team needs a winning response that can keep it on track regardless of circumstances. A great team is never defeated for long.

When you hire someone, hire someone who can help the team. Each hire should fill a need.—Bill Belichick

Belichick is well-known for drafting excellent role players who contribute unselfishly to his team. Hiring is a form of team building—perhaps the most important. In the NFL, a team's personnel is critical to its mission and success. In the NFL, "hiring" decisions are made after input from scouts and other talent evaluators, coaches, and player personnel directors. Drafting players, trading players, and new signings are most often done after solid research. The same should be true for every team.

"Individual commitment to a group effort...makes a team work, a company work, a society work, a civilization work."—Vince Lombardi

Every team member needs to be committed to the team. For many of the best coaches, the emphasis is on the team and its goals. Regardless of the huge talent and superstars that are in the market, the best teams play together as a unit.

You can learn a line from a win and a book from a defeat.—Paul Brown

Paul Brown was a legendary taskmaster and the only NFL coach to have a team named after him. He was an innovative coach for the Cleveland Browns and the Cincinnati Bengals. He was also a noteworthy high school and college coach. In the NFL, tape from each game is studied in great detail. Teams do not gloss over their losses nor do they dwell on them, rather they study them and learn from them. Much can be learned from setbacks and losses.

Principles sound so simple they are often ignored or discounted. But the NFL takes them seriously. The NFL's greats would say that a winning organization is one that focuses on need, maintains a positive approach, hires to fill needs, attracts employees who are team players, and is courageous enough to study mistakes and learn from them.

["10 Coaching Principles from the NFL" originally published as an article in the May-June 2012 Issue of *Training
Magazine.*]

FATHER BURKE MASTERS CHAPLAIN
TO CHAMPIONS

Some people believe sports can be a barrier to faith; at best
a distraction; at its worst, a kind of false god that people can
worship. But over and over again in my life, sports and faith
coexist in positive ways. Father Burke Masters's story illus-
trates this, so much so that we included his profile in *Sports
and Faith: More Stories of the Devoted and the Devout* and
put his image on the cover in 2015.

Father Masters has been busy directing vocations, participating in baseball camps, traveling to meet prospective semi-
narians, and speaking at numerous conferences. As a priest,
he says Mass, and administers the sacraments. And he is the
Chaplain of the Chicago Cubs!

Father Burke Masters was born and raised in Joliet, Illinois, the youngest of three sons of Tod and Janet Masters. His
Christian parents were not involved in church. Like many other boys, Masters wanted to become a Major League baseball
player. He was attracted to Providence Catholic High School
in New Lenox, Illinois, because of its academic and athletic
programs. At Providence, Sister Margaret Anne gave Masters
his first Bible. At Providence, Masters became intrigued by
the Catholic teaching of the Eucharist. Masters began to at-

tend Mass. One day with worshippers gathered around the altar, the priest stepped forward and placed the Eucharist on Masters's tongue before Masters could tell him he was not a Catholic. All the teaching that he had received became crystal clear. Afterwards, he joined the Catholic Church.

While attending Mississippi State University, Masters played baseball. He is remembered for his performance in one of the greatest baseball sports highlights in the school's history. It was 1990, Masters's Mississippi State team was playing Florida State in the South Regional and they were down, 8–7, in the 9th inning. Masters was red hot that day. He was 5-for-5 for the Bulldogs as he stepped up to the plate with bases loaded. Staring at a 3–1 count, Masters was thinking about taking the next pitch. A walk would tie the game, but Masters knew he had a bigger opportunity. The pitcher would want to get this one over the plate. Masters decided to play it aggressively. The ball came over the plate like a grapefruit and Masters smashed it over the left field fence to take the lead and win the game.

Overlooked in the draft by Major League Baseball, Masters earned a master's degree in Sports Administration from Ohio University and he began to work for the Kane County Cougars in Geneva, Illinois. He enjoyed the work, but he found himself being pulled toward the priesthood. He entered Mundelein Seminary and after completing his studies, he was ordained to the priesthood for the Diocese of Joliet in June of 2002. After 4 years at St. Mary's in West Chicago, he became the Vocation Director for the Diocese of Joliet.

Father Masters received Sports Faith International's Father Smyth Award that recognizes an athlete who has left the sports world for a religious vocation. Catholic Athletes for Christ reached out to Father Masters when looking for a priest to volunteer as a chaplain for the Cubs. Manager Joe Maddon is a practicing Catholic.

Masters told the Chicago Catholic newspaper: "The two things that I love to combine in my ministry is faith and sports...Never in my wildest dreams did I think I would do this with the Cubs..."

Like the Bears, the Cubs have Mass for the players and staff. Father Masters celebrates the Mass and then he makes himself available to the players. Prayer intentions are taken and he talks with players about their families.

In Chicago, the year 2016 is remembered for its faith; it's the year the Cubs beat the odds, the Billy-Goat Curse, various omens, some nay-saying fans, and much more to win the World Series. The Cubs were Champions and Father Burke Masters their Chaplain. Joe Maddon, the Manager at the helm, was no fan of omens or bad luck. And I suspect it's safe to say, the same is true for Father Burke Masters.

Masters keeps it all in perspective—as he said to *Clarion Ledger* reporter, Billy Watkins, *"Baseball is just a game. Jesus is life."*[37]

Masters has a popular blog called "Thought of the Day," in which he comments on a reading from Mass each day based on his thoughts and experiences.[38]

FREDDIE STEINMARK

Freddie Steinmark was my kind of guy. He was born in 1949. He wanted to play football for the University of Notre Dame and the Chicago Bears. Offered a scholarship to another great school, the University of Texas at Austin, he played with the Longhorns at safety and punt returner for the 1969 National Champion Season.

In "The Game of the Century" between No. 1 Texas and No. 2 Arkansas, Steinmark played on an aching left leg. Arkansas took a 14–0 lead, and held it into the fourth quarter, when Texas came from behind to win, 15–14. In the locker room, the Longhorns learned that their opponent in the Cotton Bowl, four weeks later, would be Notre Dame.

A devout Catholic, Steinmark was excited about facing quarterback Joe Theismann and the Irish. The defensive leader and signal caller would be disappointed. After he went to the doctor to get some relief from the pain in his leg, he found that he had a bone tumor just above his knee that required immediate amputation of his leg!

With his little brother Sammy at his side, Steinmark was there at the Cotton Bowl on crutches, an inspiration to his teammates and millions watching it. Texas won when with little over a minute to go they scored to take a 21–17 lead. After the game, Steinmark said, "This is the greatest day of my life." Steinmark lived another 17 months. In that time, he returned to school, coached the freshmen defensive backs, and spoke about his fight against cancer. Steinmark corresponded with Brian Piccolo who played for the Chicago Bears and was also stricken with cancer in 1969. Steinmark received the Philadelphia

Sports Writers Association's Most Courageous Athlete Award. Steinmark was inducted posthumously into the Sports Faith International Hall of Fame.[39] Steinmark is the subject of the 2015 movie "My All American." He is also featured in *Freddie Steinmark: Faith, Family, Football,* by Bower Yousse and Thomas J. Cryan; and *Courage Beyond the Game* by Jim Dent.

MENTORED BY FATHER MECONI

Father David Meconi, S.J. grew up in Pau Pau, Michigan. He did his undergraduate work at Hope College in Holland, Michigan. He is a member of the Chicago Province of the Society of Jesus; holds the pontifical license in Patristics from the University of Innsbruck; and holds the Doctorate in Ecclesiastical History from Oxford.[40] He is a professor of early Church history at Saint Louis University.

Father Meconi gave a series of eight conferences at Bellarmine Jesuit Retreat House in Barrington. It was for a men's silent retreat that I attended. Father Meconi was inspiring. Here are 10 thoughts that I want to share with you from his presentation:

1. Life can be beautiful, if we choose to do the good.
2. True love is made in the goodness and likeness of God.
3. A father's true job is to get us to the true Father.
4. The beginning of grace is allowing the Lord to be our savior.
5. Pride is when we give ourselves perfections that we don't really have.
6. Let God show you who you were meant to be.

7. If you want to know how to live, you have to know how to die.
8. We need to stand up for people who are being ridiculed.
9. There is nothing ordinary about Christian life.
10. Find God in all things.

TOM MONAGHAN

Tom Monaghan's success came from working for future gains, unimaginable hard work, and fortitude. After 38 years of running Dominos, Monaghan sold controlling interest in the company to Bain Capital.[41]

Since that time, Monaghan has focused on philanthropic interests. Monaghan was honored with the Pope John Paul II Family Fidelity Award in 1988, the Marine Corp Leatherneck Award in 1990, the Proudly Pro-Life Award in 2000, and the Sports Faith Hall of Fame award in 2010. Whether it's building a chapel at the Domino's headquarters or fighting the government mandate to force organizations to provide birth control coverage in health insurance coverage, Monaghan continues to take a strong stand on issues involving faith.

Monaghan created the Ave Maria Foundation to direct his philanthropic efforts in a hands-on way. What followed was Ave Maria Institute in Ypsilanti that would become Ave Maria College, Ave Maria School of Law, Ave Maria Radio, and the Thomas More Law Center—offering legal aid for people of faith who face religious freedom challenges. Monaghan also created Legatus, an organization of wealthy Catholic business leaders. He is the founder and greatest benefactor of Ave Maria University in Florida which was established in 2003. Monaghan currently holds the position of chancellor. Monaghan has also been active in supporting Catholic work and institutions in Nicaragua and Honduras.

Monaghan has received honorary degrees from twelve universities around the country, and in March of 2000, he was named an Honorary Fellow of Magdalene College within Britain's University of Cambridge.

RESOLUTION FOR TOM MONAGHAN

STATE OF ILLINOIS

COUNTY OF LAKE

RESOLUTION

WHEREAS, Thomas Stephen Monaghan was born March 25, 1937, in Ann Arbor, Michigan, and

WHEREAS, Tom was in the United States Marine Corps from 1956 through 1959, and

WHEREAS, Tom was a founder of Domino's Pizza, and

WHEREAS, Tom married Marjorie Zybach in 1962, and

WHEREAS, they have four daughters, 10 grandchildren, and two great-grandchildren, and

WHEREAS, Tom was the owner of the Detroit Tigers when they won the championship in 1984, and

WHEREAS, Tom was the founder of Legatus, Thomas More Law Center, Ave Maria Foundation, Ave Maria Law School, Ave Maria Radio, Ave Maria University, and Ave Maria Mutual Funds, and

WHEREAS, Tom flies coach and sits in the middle seat so that he can evangelize to the people who are sitting on either side of him, and

WHEREAS, Tom is a Sports Faith Hall of Famer.

NOW THEREFORE BE IT RESOLVED that the Chicago Bears adopt this Resolution to honor and hold in high esteem Tom Monaghan.

Adopted the 25th day of March, 2017.

SAINT LUCY FEAST DAY

Saint Lucy and Her Feast Day

Saint Lucy of Syracuse, Sicily, also known as Santa Lucia, is the patron saint of eye ailments. Her feast day is December 13. Saint Lucy lived in the late 3rd and early 4th centuries. She, along with Saint Agnes, Saint Agatha and Saint Cecilia, are known as the four great virgin martyrs of the early church. In the 6th century, her name was added to the Canon of the Mass. At the end of the 7th century, the English Bishop Saint Aldhelm of Sherborne wrote about her.[42]

Devotion to Saint Lucy is not only strong in her native Sicily, but throughout the Christian world and especially in Protestant Scandinavia where they celebrate the feast day of "Santa Lucia" with great devotion and affection for the saint. The feast day falls close to Christmas and the celebrations in some way evoke the Christian Holiday. Young girls sometimes wear a wreath of candles on their heads as tradition holds that Santa Lucia did to see better while serving poor Christians hiding in catacombs. In some Scandinavian homes, the oldest daughter dresses in a white gown on the feast day and wakes up family members and serves them Santa Lucia Day sweets. In some parishes, a special Mass procession on Santa Lucia's feast day is held with young girls carrying candles and the lead girl wearing a wreath of lights.

Saint Lucy's Life

Saint Lucy's father died when she was young and her mother, Eutychia, suffered from chronic hemorrhaging. Lucy had been engaged to a pagan, perhaps so that she could be supported in some way given the state of her mother. Eutychia and Lucy traveled to the tomb of Saint Agatha in Catania about 39 miles up the coast to pray and ask for the Saint's intercession for improved health. Eutychia was cured. Lucy then convinced her mother to allow her to dedicate herself to God as a virgin (as she had secretly done). She then sold her dowry and gave the money to the poor. When her suitor was stung with rejection, he revealed Lucy's Christianity to the authorities and she was sentenced to serve in a brothel. When the soldiers laid hands on her to take her away, they could not move her and attempted several debaucheries—eventually blinding her. Her wounds killed her in 304 AD. While her death was unimaginably brutal for modern Christians to contemplate—her focus on Jesus, her faith, and her feast day have given millions a beautiful Christian experience and example.

PILLARS OF THE NFL

QUIZ—PILLARS OF THE NFL

Questions

1. Who was the only coach and owner who was present at the beginning of the NFL and helped bring it into the modern TV age? The only man who could rightfully be called: "Father of the NFL?"

2. Who brought football coaching into the modern age? Didn't care about skin color, but cared about most every detail of running a football team. He ran his organization like a business. He was successful at every level of football coaching from high school to college to professional. This

coach learned about timeliness and discipline from his father who was a railroad man.

3. Tough man for a tough city. Never thought the press needed to know everything about a man's personal life. Thought players and coaches needed a life outside of football—he had many interests himself. Grew up in Cleveland. Who was this coach who led many Hall of Famers to a dynasty in the 1970s?

4. Little man who managed two superstar quarterbacks in two different cities to NFL championships. His people were Quakers. He worked towards results, not notoriety. Who was this cradle of coaches favorite who lived until age 91?

5. Tough coach who was influenced by his tight knit family and the Jesuits at Fordham. Another coach who embraced diversity and mandated respect for everyone in the locker room. In fact, he mandated a lot of things. His team practiced fundamentals until they knew them in their sleep. He was so tough that some players said they hated him while playing for him, but all seemed to love him for what he helped them become. Who was this coach who created a small city dynasty in the 1960s?

6. A master at coaching quarterbacks—this man was good with his fists as a young man, but he looked like he walked off the country club to the sideline at football games. Who was this man whom many called the "Genius?"

7. Nebraska farm boy who was himself one of the top professional players when he coached and played to four championships in the 1920s for three different teams. He did

not see a long-term future in professional football so he went back eventually to his family farm outside of Lincoln. Who was he?

8. His father was in law enforcement in North Carolina. The family moved out west to California where he went to school and began his coaching career. He was a master at adaptation and although he had learned Don Coryell's wide open offensive schemes, he based his game plan on the talent at hand. When he and his coaches prepared for games, they worked incredibly long hours developing master plans for victories. He was also a master at making adjustments during a game and was always willing to toss out things that weren't working and incorporate the new. This coach was super competitive in everything he did. Who was this man who is also a member of the professional auto racing community?

9. His father was an exceptional football thinker who settled into a life time of scouting at the Naval Academy. This coach has always displayed a military mindset that mandates that each player focuses on doing his job and the team is always more important than any player. Although his coaching approach is somewhat old fashioned in our Super Star age, he is the most successful NFL coach of the 21st century. Who is he?

10. A superb athlete and demanding coach, he competed against George Halas in the early days of professional football through World War II. He had a great eye for talent and brought some of the greatest football players of the era to his small city club. Newspapers from all over the world covered

his David and Goliath sports story that featured a small city team winning championships against the big city teams. Who was this man?

Answers

1. George Papa Bear Halas is the father of the NFL.
2. Paul Brown saw the importance of discipline in most every aspect of running a football team. He could have run General Motors.
3. Chuck Noll was the Pied Piper of Hall of Fame players at Pittsburgh and the perfect coach for the Steel City.
4. Weeb Ewbank lived a joyful life and was always prepared to let his players take the top billing in the papers. But he was vastly underestimated as a tremendous coaching talent and manager of men who built teams from the ground up.
5. Vince Lombardi wanted his men to become the best they could be and he drove them to it. Like the Jesuits, he believed each person's talent should be developed for maximum use.
6. Bill Walsh was a dashing figure on the side lines and he knew how to develop quarterbacks. He focused on what his players could do and coached them to become consistent. Despite his outward appearance, Walsh was a boxer all his life and he took every loss personally.

7.   Guy Chamberlin stepped off a Nebraska farm to become one of the best athletes and coaches in professional football. He played end on offense and defense. He was extremely fast and although the early football's bloated rugby ball shape made it difficult to develop a passing game, the end around was used liberally—he excelled at it. On defense he was known as a disruptor of the first order. He was tall, lean, and mean on the field.

8.   Joe Gibbs just seemed to be smarter, more hardworking, and more adaptable than most other coaches. If there was a plan that could spring victory from defeat, Gibbs was generally the man who could come up with it.

9.   Belichick has a military no-nonsense coaching persona that has made old fashion management schemes seem new again. Everyone in Belichick's Patriot's organization is responsible for their piece of the pie—no excuses.

10.   Curly Lambeau's name is well known because the Packers named their stadium after him. He learned coaching on the job and he managed and willed his team to greatness. He was a scrapper. Few men were his coaching equal.

BRONKO NAGURSKI WHEATIES CEREAL BOX

Obey the Personal Conduct Policy.

Introduction

Athletes and coaches need self-control and discipline. This is a problem for some. But those who practice these can be rewarded. The football player who keeps his cool can ride out a close game for a win. Many of the best athletes perform under pressure while others around them melt. Jack Nicklaus was exceptional at this. Mohammed Ali was a fiery talker, but disciplined in the ring.

Pro Football Coach Paul Brown liked good men and he wanted no part of thugs. Vince Lombardi wanted his players tuned in and focused for the good of the team. He often fined players for their indiscretions. He brought some of them to Mass with him. Coach George Halas faced problems with discipline head on—even when it involved the monstrous 6-foot-8 Doug Atkins who was said to be "whooping it up" in a tavern after hours. After a "conversation" in the bar, the two men settled their differences and called it a night.

The meaning of this commandment is *follow the rules of good behavior.*

Nagurski Junior's Lesson from Dad

Ranked as one of the top football players in NFL history, Hall of Famer Bronko Nagurski played fullback and linebacker for the Bears from 1930-1937. During those years, the Bears won championships in 1932 and 1933. Nagurski came back in the war-year of 1943 to help the Bears win another championship. Nagurski had the size, speed, and toughness to play in any era.

Pay was modest during the 1930s. The Depression was on and Halas had almost lost the team in 1931 when he had to pay his partner, Dutch Sternaman, for his share of the team. Nagurski was a national celebrity and he turned to professional wresting in 1938.

In January 1990, I went to Bronko Nagurski's funeral. The sign at the airport declared that International Falls, Minnesota, was "The Icebox of the Nation." Electrical plugs stick out of car grills for engine block heaters that plug into outlets at stores, hotels, and other outdoor lots to keep cars starting.

The Holiday Inn had a Bronko Nagurski Room. A plaque proclaimed that he was an All-American on offense and defense in 1929; all-time All-American; all-pro; football hall of fame member; and the all-time greatest football player.

The Riverfront Room for dining had a helpful, large thermometer right outside the window. During the dinner on Friday, January 12, the temperature was 6.

The Nagurskis had a gathering at Bronko's house. There were scrapbooks and piles of pictures available for people to study. The tiny, gold footballs from the Chicago Bears championships in 1932, 1933, and 1943 were there, too.

Bronko was on a Wheaties box.[43] He was also the leader of a touring basketball team. In 1946, he was an assistant football coach at UCLA.

Bronko Junior told this story.

"I was a smart-aleck high school kid.

"After we got home from a football game one day, my father asked me how I thought I had played. I said, 'Pretty good; we won didn't we?"

"He asked me, 'How was your stance?'"

"I said, 'Fine.'"

"He said, 'Get in it.'"

"He asked me, 'Are you ready?'"

"Before I was finished saying 'yeah,' I was up against the wall. After that it was always 'yes, sir' and 'no, sir.'"

Bronko Junior lettered 3 years as a tackle at the University of Notre Dame. Then he played seven seasons for Hamilton in the Canadian Football League.

The funeral was at Saint Thomas Aquinas Church on Saturday, January 13. Six grandchildren led the prayers of the faithful, one at a time. Four other grandchildren presented the gifts. There are usually no burials in International Falls in the winter. An exception was made for Nagurski. He was named after Saint Bronko, who was the patron saint of fullbacks.

Tom Waddle: All-Madden Wide Receiver and Fan Favorite

Tom Waddle graduated from Boston College in 1989 with a degree in finance. A 3-year starter for the Boston College Eagles, he finished as the school's all-time leading receiver. In 1989, Waddle received the National Football Foundation Hall of Fame Scholar Athlete Award, given to top Division I student athletes.

From 1989 to 1994, Waddle, a self-described "lunch bucket kind of guy," played for the Chicago Bears.[44] Waddle faced many setbacks on his way to the Bears' lineup when he was cut several times from the squad. Waddle literally "kept the faith" and made the team. Waddle earned a spot in the Sports Faith Hall of Fame.

In six Bears' seasons, he caught 173 passes for 2100 yards and 9 touchdowns. Many were clutch catches in heavy traffic—earning him the admiration of one special fan, former NFL Coach and sports broadcaster John Madden. In 1991, Waddle was selected for the All-Madden Team. Waddle played with heart and determination. He is a favorite of Bears' fans and for good reason. Film clips of Waddle remind fans of his fearless performances. His popularity followed him after his football playing career ended.

Today, Waddle is a superb National NFL analyst for ESPN and he is co-host of the popular Waddle and Silvy show also on ESPN. Waddle is also featured on ABC 7 Television in Chicago on a segment called "Waddle's World." Intelligence, sense of humor, and an effort to avoid taking himself too seriously are his on-air distinguishing features.

Tom Waddle

He was an All-State receiver for Moeller High.
Through it all he was a quiet guy.
He was an All-East receiver for Boston College.
His finance degree noted good knowledge.
In 1989, he signed with the Chicago Bears.
He was cut three times and he still ran the stairs.
He was knocked out of games, but not for long.
His courage and great plays made the Bears strong.
Tom Waddle was a great gamer.
Now he is a Sports Faith Hall of Famer.

Gird Your Loins

1 Kings 18:46, "But the hand of the Lord was on Elijah, who girded up his clothing and ran before Ahab as far as the approaches to Jezreel."

Job 38:3, "Gird up your loins now, like a man; I will question you, and you tell me the answers!"

Jeremiah 1:17, "But do you gird your loins; stand up and tell them all that I command you. Be not crushed on their account, as though I would leave you crushed before them."

Luke 12:35, "Gird your loins and light your lamps and be like servants who await their master's return from a wedding, ready to open immediately when he comes and knocks."

Ephesians 6:14, "So stand fast with your loins girded in truth, clothed with righteousness as a breastplate, and your feet shod in readiness for the gospel of peace."

1 Peter 1:13, "Therefore, gird up the loins of your mind, live soberly, and set your hopes completely on the grace to be brought to you at the revelation of Jesus Christ."

MARTIN SHEEN'S VIETNAM EXORCISM

In our last Sports and Faith book called *Pilgrimage*, I wrote about a movie called "The Way." In it, Martin Sheen plays an ophthalmologist whose free-spirited son, played by Emilio Estévez (Sheen's own son), dies on his first day of pilgrimage. The Way, or more formally, "El Camino de Santiago de Compostela," commands physical sacrifice on the long journey over the Pyrenees and across northern Spain to the Cathedral of Saint James.[45] Sheen takes the place of his son on the Camino and finishes a trek of discovery and faith. Viewers come with him. The movie shows a spiritual journey that has motivated many Catholics to take their own trips of discovery.

In 1976-1977, a much younger Sheen acted in "Apocalypse Now," an intense movie about a different journey directed by Francis Coppola. Taking place during the Vietnam War, many

consider "Apocalypse Now" Sheen's most memorable performance. In the movie, Sheen plays a stressed out Special Forces
Officer, Captain Willard, who is sent into the jungle in Cam-
bodia on a secret mission to locate and kill a renegade Colonel
Kurtz, played by Marlon Brando. As Willard travels through the
jungle, his character becomes more and more tormented.

Sheen identified closely with the role of Captain Willard and the actor's real-life personal battles boiled over during filming. The tormented performer suffered a heart attack.
Alone at the time in his housing, Sheen crawled out into the
night and found help to get him to a hospital. The experience
became a kind of exorcism for Sheen and he was able to kill
off his own demons, face his own problems with alcohol, and
renew his faith. For Sheen it was a kind of death and rebirth.
At 36-years old, Sheen went back to the Catholic Church that
he had left many years before. Sheen said he recalled something he had forgotten: "love is the foundation of happiness.
Love of family, love of people, and love of God."[46] Sheen had
successful bypass surgery in 2015.

LIVES OF GREAT MEN

When my father was a boy, he came in from grade school one
day for lunch. His great grandfather asked, "What did you
learn in school today young man?"

My father replied, "Nothing sir."

His great grandfather said, "Oh nothing. We must never
have that. Fetch the Longfellow."

So, that day, before my father got lunch, he learned that
"Lives of great men all remind us
We can make our lives sublime,
And, departing, leave behind us
Foot prints on the sands of time."[47]

JORDAN ROBERTS

Father Smyth was an All-American basketball player for the University of Notre Dame. After he had played a year of professional basketball for the Saint Louis Hawks and the Harlem Globetrotters, he entered the seminary to become a priest.

In 2009, Father Smyth became a Sports Faith Hall of Famer. Sports Faith also created the Father Smyth Award in honor of the man whose life bears testimony to the world-changing power of combining the virtues and influence of sports with mountain-moving faith. This honor is awarded to an outstanding athlete or coach interested in pursuing a religious vocation. In 2017, the Father Smyth Award was given to Jordan Roberts.

Sheridan, Wyoming native Jordan Roberts had a football scholarship at South Dakota. His teammates encouraged him to take advantage of student Bible Study through the Fellowship of Catholic University Students (FOCUS), the Catholic Campus outreach program. Then they encouraged him to attend a Catholic conference for college students in Orlando. After he had been meeting with the chaplain at South Dakota's Newman Center, Jordan decided to enter Saint John Vianney Seminary at the University of Saint Thomas in Saint Paul.

At the seminary, Jordan was encouraged to play football for the University of Saint Thomas. He was a superb running back for the Tommies.

For the South Dakota Coyotes in 2010-2012, Roberts accumulated 1,001 all-purpose yards and three touchdowns in 21 games. With the Tommies, Roberts recorded his best statistical season in 2015 when he broke the Saint Thomas single-season rushing record with 2,092 yards. He became the first player in the Minnesota Intercollegiate Athletic Conference to score 36 touchdowns in a season and earned both NCAA Division III Offensive Player of the Year and first-team All-America honors.[48]

After I had contacted Jordan about receiving the Father Smyth Award, he told me that he grew up as an absolute die hard Chicago Bears' fan. He is *"incredibly grateful and humbled for this great honor and recognition."*

JOHN GAGLIARDI

John Gagliardi retired after his 64th season as head football coach (most in history) and 60th season as head coach of Saint John's University in Collegeville in 2012. Gagliardi is a legend in college coaching.

Gagliardi was the first active head coach inducted into the College Football Hall of Fame. He was the 2009 American Football Coaches' Association (AFCA) Amos Alonzo Stagg Award recipient and the 2007 Liberty Mutual Division III

Coach of the Year after his team's perfect 14–0 season earning an NCAA Division III championship.

Gagliardi is the winningest college football coach of all-time finishing with a 489–138–11 collegiate career record and a 465–132–10 record at Saint John's University.

Gagliardi began his coaching career at age 16 when as team captain he took over for his high school coach at Trinidad Catholic (Colorado) who was drafted to serve in World War II. His first college coaching position was at Carroll College (Montana) where he led his team to three conference titles in four seasons. Meanwhile, Saint John's University in Collegeville, Minnesota, had not won a conference title in 15 years. Gagliardi was asked to take over the program in 1953 and never looked back. Initially, he also coached hockey and track.

After 60 seasons, Gagliardi's teams set the standard for excellence. They won four national championships, reached the national semifinals six times, won an incredible 30 conference titles, and appeared in 58 post-season games. In June 2006, Gagliardi was inducted into the National Association of Collegiate Directors (NACDA) Hall of Fame. In 2010, Gagliardi was inducted as the Sports Faith International Coach of the Year. In the coach's honor, for 25 years, Jostens and the Saint John University J-Club has been awarding the Gagliardi Trophy to the nation's outstanding Division III player.[49]

In addition to achieving an incredible record, Gagliardi created an environment of fun and high expectations. He concentrated on methods and practices that won games.

His coaching methods are described as a series of "Winning with Nos:"

    No blocking sleds or dummies

    No scholarships

    No compulsory weightlifting program

    No whistles

    No "coach"–players called him John

    No tackling in practice – players wear shorts or sweats

    No long practices–an hour and a half or less

John Gagliardi died on October 7, 2018, at age 91. Will there ever be another college football coach like Gagliardi?

FRANK AMATO

FRANK AMATO

Loyola Academy alumni know the meaning of Latin word "Amato"—one who is loved. They love Frank Amato, the legendary coach and administrator.

Coach Frank Amato approaches every job with confidence and vigor. He tells everyone they can either participate or compete, and competing is what it is all about. Community, care, compassion are critical for educators and coaches, but you also need to have a "great desire to excel." In the Jesuit tradition, Amato's efforts were for the "Greater Glory of God"—he focused on each individual and their potential in a team setting.

Out of high school, Amato was headed off to Notre Dame, but when the Unites States entered World War II, he joined the Marines—serving in the Pacific theater.[50] Back to Notre Dame in 1948, he played football his freshman year. Amato graduated in 1952 and went right to work for Norfolk High School in Virginia, where he was a Physical Education instructor, head football coach, head track coach, and head basketball coach. When Father English at Loyola High School asked him to take a job in 1966, he was told they just wanted a football and track coach, but they expected 60-40 seasons with Catholic League Championships to follow. Amato took the job.[51]

Amato coached football for 14 seasons and track for 47 years, retiring in 2013. His track teams won 19 Catholic League indoor championships and 12 outdoor. Thousands of students and dozens of coaches have passed through Amato's program at Loyola. He was honored with the Sports Faith International All-Star Catholic High School Life Time Achievement Award and he and his wife, Alice, were given the Reverend Daniel A. Lord, SJ, Award for Distinguished Service in the Cause of Youth. Amato was inducted into the Loyola Catholic Athletic Hall of Fame, Chicago Catholic League Hall of Fame, and Illinois Track and Cross Country Coaches Association Hall of Fame. He received the National Coach of the Year by the National High School Athletic Coaches Association. Loyola Academy's new track was renamed the Amato Track in honor of the Coach.

FATHER AND SONS

My father obeyed the law of gravity. He considered it a privilege to help his father in the garden. He never talked back to his mother. My father chose my mother. He renounced Satan and all his works and all his empty promises.

My son, Ed, met Elizabeth at a Pro Life Dinner. After they had been dating for a month, Ed said to her, *"Just so you know, if I ever have a son, he'll be named after my father."* In 2013, they got married. In 2015, their daughter, Grace, was born. In 2016, their son, Pat, was born. In 2018, their daughter, Charlotte, was born.

When my son James's age was in single digits, I asked him if I could please call him Jim. He responded, "Can I have a dog?"

James applied to seven colleges. My plan for him was to have a semester at each college. For the eighth semester, I would home school him and he would be valedictorian.

After he had earned a master's degree and after he had become a certified public accountant, he ran away from home.

My plan for my sons was that if they did not become priests, they would get married and have children and we would all live together in the same house like the Waltons. Children don't always do what their parents want them to do.

And yet, children are a blessing. They grow up and they get married. If they are blessed with children, we hope and trust that the parents will provide accountability and encouragement for the children.

In preparation for marrying Emily, Jim developed physically, socially, culturally, and spiritually. I am grateful to Jim for being my son. I am grateful to Emily for accepting Jim's invitation.

The Bears have an outreach to the Chicago Public Schools. The players and I visit schools and we talk about the importance of education and a healthy lifestyle. The program for boys is called BAM: becoming a man. We have a PIES check in: Physically, Intellectually, Emotionally, and Spiritually. Here is my check in.

Physically, I'm working out six days a week. Even God took a day off. Workouts are recess. Intellectually, I wrote this book, my sixth, *Worthwhile Struggle*. Emotionally, I'm thrilled to speaking at various events. It is better than talking to myself. Spiritually, I go to Church and Bible Study and I have daily devotions. I'm checking in.

Chicago Bears' Joe Fortunato

Out of Mississippi State, the 6-foot-1, 225 pound speedy fullback and linebacker, Joe Fortunato, participated in both the Senior Bowl and the East-West Shrine game. Selected by the Chicago Bears in the seventh round of the NFL Draft, Fortunato spent 12 seasons at linebacker in the NFL. He joined the Bears for the 1955 season after serving in the military.

He was a four-time All-Pro selection and a five-time Pro Bowl pick who was a member of the Bears' 1963 Championship team. He was a member of the NFL's All-Decade Team for the 1950s. Many believe he should be in the Pro Football Hall of Fame. An assistant coach for George Halas's final season coaching in 1967, Fortunato died on November 6, 2017.

Fortunato was enshrined into the Mississippi State football Ring of Honor; he is also a member of the National Italian American Sports Hall of Fame. After football, he operated Big Joe Oil Company and lived in Natchez, Mississippi.

He was the founder of the Joe Fortunato Celebrity Golf Classic which provides funds to seven area high schools scholar-athletes scholarships. Fortunato helped fund the Joe Fortunato Scholarship given to one girl student-athlete and one boy student-athlete at Indian Creek High School.

The generous college and NFL star also set up a scholarship given out each year to a student at Mississippi State. According to Chicago Bears Chairman, George McCaskey:

"Joe Fortunato was not only a great player for the Chicago Bears, including being a part of our 1963 Championship

at Wrigley Field, he was a key figure in one of the greatest linebacker trios in Bears history alongside Hall of Famer Bill George and Larry Morris."

BRENNON NORRIS

Fortunato Scholarship recipient, Indian Creek's Brennon Norris, finished with 2,005 passing yards and 14 touchdowns in 2017. Norris also set school records for completions and yardage in a single game.

RESOLUTION FOR JOE FORTUNATO AND BRENNON NORRIS

STATE OF ILLINOIS

COUNTY OF LAKE

RESOLUTION

WHEREAS, Joe Fortunato was born on March 28, 1930 in Mingo Junction, Ohio, and

WHEREAS, Joe Fortunato played fullback and linebacker for Mississippi State University, and made All-American in 1951, and

WHEREAS, Joe Fortunato was a 7th round draft choice of the Bears in 1952, and

WHEREAS, Joe Fortunato played linebacker for the Bears from 1955 through 1966, and

WHEREAS, Joe Fortunato played in five Pro Bowls, and

WHEREAS, Joe Fortunato was All-Pro four times, and

WHEREAS, Joe Fortunato made the NFL 1950s All-Decade Team, and

WHEREAS, Joe Fortunato played on the Bears' 1963 Championship team, and

WHEREAS, Joe Fortunato was a Bears' assistant coach in 1967 and 1968, and

WHEREAS, Brennon Norris is the 2017 Indian Creek Joe Fortunato Player of the Year.

NOW THEREFORE BE IT RESOLVED that the Chicago Bears adopt this resolution to honor and hold Joe Fortunato and Brennon Norris in high esteem.

Adopted the 14th day of November, 2017.

AN UNDELIVERABLE SERMON

The Scripture says,
We were created
In God's Image.
Our bodies are temples
Of The Holy Spirit.
Some of us need
To downsize.

SAINT KEVIN OF THE NETTLES

For the Irish, their stories of saints and religious figures are often accepted on faith. Many Irish believe the true nature of the person or the deed is crucial. The poetry of the situation holds sway. They tell a good story and remember it. And so they hold their faith close to their hearts in everyday life.

Glendalough in the Wicklow Mountains is famous for its monastic school and its founder, Saint Kevin (of the Nettles). Born near Rathdrum at the end of the 5th century, Kevin means fair-begotten and it is said he was the first man named Kevin. Saint Kevin was tutored at first by Saint Petroc of Cornwall on the Scriptures. Then he studied under his uncle, Saint Eugenius, who had studied in the famous British monastery of Rosnat.[52]

THE NETTLES

According to Irish tradition, young Kevin was a handsome youth. One day he was followed into the woods by a young maiden. When he realized, he was in danger of committing a sin, he threw himself into a bed of nettles—thus earning the nickname—Kevin of the Nettles. Some sources suggest that he is associated with nettles because he ate them as people sometimes have done.[53]

NOT ALLOWED TO LIVE AS A HERMIT

Kevin retired into the wilds of the Glendalough valley, where he lived in a cave by himself until holy men and others gathered around him. He was asked to build a monastery. And like other such men, his humility and self-denial attracted disciples and a school of learning. From this monastery came others, and around it grew a town. Saint Kevin served as abbot for several years, but once the monastery was well-established, he withdrew once again to live as a hermit. Four years later, he returned to Glendalough at a monk's request and served as abbot until his death at age 120.

Saint Kevin was a great protector of animals. Many of Saint Kevin's miracles involve nature and animals. His feast day is June 3rd. He died in 618 and received his canonization in 1903.

Seamus Heaney wrote a poem based on Irish-Catholic tradition called "Saint Kevin and the Blackbird."[54] A blackbird landed on Saint Kevin's hand—the bird laid its eggs in his hand. The kind saint holds the bird until the eggs hatch and the young birds are ready to leave.[55]

Saint Kevin and the Blackbird

And then there was St Kevin and the blackbird.
The saint is kneeling, arms stretched out, inside
His cell, but the cell is narrow, so

One turned-up palm is out the window, stiff
As a crossbeam, when a blackbird lands
And lays in it and settles down to nest.

Kevin feels the warm eggs, the small breast, the tucked
Neat head and claws and, finding himself linked
Into the network of eternal life,

Is moved to pity: now he must hold his hand
Like a branch out in the sun and rain for weeks
Until the young are hatched and fledged and flown.

And since the whole thing's imagined anyhow,
Imagine being Kevin. Which is he?
Self-forgetful or in agony all the time

From the neck on out down through his hurting forearms?
Are his fingers sleeping? Does he still feel his knees?
Or has the shut-eyed blank of underearth

Crept up through him? Is there distance in his head?
Alone and mirrored clear in love's deep river,
'To labour and not to seek reward,' he prays,

A prayer his body makes entirely
For he has forgotten self, forgotten bird
And on the riverbank forgotten the river's name.

SPORTS AND FAITH; STORIES OF THE DEVOTED AND THE DEVOUT

Quiz—Bears' Head Coaches

Questions

1. Raised in San Diego, which Bears' head coach played football at San Diego State and he had so much energy he did this (California thing) between two-a-day practices?

2. A Bears' head coach had this to say about Chuck Noll: "I think he's the greatest guy I've ever been around. He is very calm, very technique—and fundamental-oriented. He is not a screamer. He wasn't up or down. I think his biggest thing is that he was the same guy every day." Who was it?

3. Which Bears' head coach played quarterback at the University of Minnesota behind Tony Dungy?

4. Which Bears' head coach graduated from the University of Miami Law School?

5. Which Bears' head coach has been lauded by the quarterbacks who played under him crediting him with greatly improving their confidence and play?

6. One day during Bears' Training Camp, Head Coach George Halas called his grandchildren over to pass out some pocket money. This Bear's future head coach suddenly appeared to ask: "Hey coach how about some of that for me?" Halas replied, "never mind!" Who was it?

7. Which Bears' head coach was in charge when the Bears slaughtered the Packers, 61–7, December 7, 1980? No doubt it was a day that would live in infamy in Green Bay.

8. Which Bears' head coach was in charge when the Bears beat the Eagles in a game that would become known as the Fog Bowl?

9. In 1968, which Bears' head coach replaced George Halas when Halas retired from coaching?

10. Who was the Bears' Head Coach when they won the NFL Championship in 1963?

Answers

1. John Fox went surfing.
2. John Fox had worked for Chuck Noll and was a big fan.
3. Mark Trestman was behind Dungy.
4. Mark Trestman is a lawyer.
5. Mark Trestman is a great quarterback coach.
6. Halas turned down Mike Ditka.
7. Neill Armstrong will always be loved in Chicago for this game.
8. Mike Ditka coached a number of notable games including the Fog Bowl in 1988.
9. Jim Dooley took over from Papa Bear.
10. The NFL Championship in 1963 was the last one that George Halas won as head coach.

FRANK FAUNCE AND SON

WORK FOR THE GOOD OF THE LEAGUE.

INTRODUCTION

We like to belong. We belong to a family. We have friends. We belong to churches, clubs, and political parties. To belong is a basic human need and the best of us work for the good of the groups to which we belong.

Many Americans have lost their sense of belongingness. Many describe it as a crisis. Maybe it's a result of our virtual associations? Maybe it's our focus on technology? But those who have lost a sense of belonging, can feel isolated—from family, friends, community, and church.

Important personal associations cannot be adequately replaced by social media. We need to talk to people directly and exchange ideas and thoughts. We need to ask each other questions in real time and answer questions as well. Every nuance in speaking and listening that occurs only in person, needs to occur. And we need to care about each other.

The loss of personal associations today is not new. After the Civil War, the fighting men had lived through hell, but they had achieved a sense of comradery. Battle-weary comrades became a brotherhood. When they returned home there was a void. Eventually, they joined clubs and sought association with others.

For Catholics in the mid-19th century, war veterans were not the only ones experiencing a problem with belonging. There was a large mix of immigrants who had come from Ireland and other places. Many Catholic leaders were concerned that by joining some of the "Protestant" clubs that were being created, they might find discrimination and perhaps even lose their faith. Catholic parents were also concerned about their children and how they would face discrimination in the public schools and lose their Catholic identity. So Catholic schools were opened up with the tremendous support of the parishioners—and sometimes with help from the "old country" as well. Various church organizations were created that offered faith, fellowship, athletics, and even theater. In the Irish communities especially, some of the church groups were also promoting abstinence as alcohol problems were rampant.

In time, there were fewer threats as Americans were more accepting. Still, 100 years later during the Kennedy-Nixon campaign, there was a great deal of mistrust among Americans of different faiths. It exists today as well.

And while it is important to maintain our faith and roots, it is also important to value much of the philosophy of self-determination, independence, and hard work that was so ably fostered by our Protestant foundations in America. These foundations helped make this country great. And regardless of the faiths we bring with us when we land, we need to appreciate the solid basis on which we stand and cherish it going forward.

In America, there will always be a struggle about what we hang onto as a nation because it is just and good, and what we discard as a nation, because it is selfish, wrong, and cruel. The fundamental principles of our faith are the fundamental principles of our nation. When John F. Kennedy said, "Ask not what your country can do for you, but ask what you can do for your country," that was a fundamental principle of America. Americans should not be focused on only their own interests. At the same time, Americans believe that charity cannot be commanded. And so it's important to work for a just society where all people have an equal opportunity.

Work for the good of the league means to **work for the good of all.**

"There's Still a Lot of Good Things Happening in the World."

Chicago Bears' tight end Zach Miller returned to Halas Hall on Monday December 11, 2017, after a season-ending knee injury occurred on October 29th in the Chicago Bears–New Orleans Saints game. The injury nearly resulted in the amputation of his left leg—much more severe than a dislocated knee injury might suggest to football fans. Miller suffered a tear to an artery which quickly became the focus on his treatment. Surgery on a popliteal artery behind the knee was required immediately to restore blood flow. In June 2018, things looked much brighter as Miller and the Bears happily agreed on a contract that extended Miller's presence in the locker room and on the playing fields. Miller has frequently been described as one of the best men in the locker room. In 2016, he received the Brian Piccolo Award, an honor given to players who exemplify the courage, loyalty, teamwork, dedication, and sense of humor of the late Bears running back.

In the December news conference, Miller described his experience following the recent knee injury:

"That was very real, a couple wrong turns away from actually happening. I had a ton of care, a lot of people helping me out throughout that entire process. But we were a couple minutes away from having that be real.

"I remember, before I got into the emergency surgery, the last thing I was telling the doctors was 'Please, save my leg!'"

Miller injured the leg seemingly making a touchdown catch although it was overruled by the refs who said he failed to maintain possession throughout the process. Miller called the outpouring of support a life-changing event, and singled out Bears Chairman George McCaskey.

"That guy's been awesome, and that'll be a memory I'll keep forever."

Miller talked about his wife's and family's support, as well as his teammates. He mentioned how he has heard from people all over the world, who have reached out to him. Pointing out that we hear so much about the bad things happening, Miller said, *"There's still a lot of good things happening in the world."*

Regardless of the surgeries, the knee's structure remains solid although Miller suffered a foot fracture in 2016, a torn Achilles in 2012 and a shoulder injury in 2011. [56]

Always an athlete, Miller has talked about a comeback: *"I've been a football player my whole life. I would love to play football..."*

ALEX RUIZ

Since suffering the 2017 injury, Zach Miller has sought out pros who've had similar injuries. Miller has also been in contact with a Temecula, California, Linfield Christian High School football player, Alex Ruiz, who faced amputation following a similar injury during the 2017 season. Always upbeat, quarterback Ruiz has inspired Miller and Miller has offered support to Ruiz.

DREW BREES AND ALEX RUIZ

New Orleans Saints quarterback Drew Brees is Ruiz's QB idol. San Diego-based Challenged Athletes Foundation is the charity partner of a co-ed flag football league, Football "N" America, which Brees co-founded. The league funded a grant for the CAF to provide a prosthetic leg for the young quarterback. On May 11, 2018, Brees surprised Ruiz with a prosthetic leg at a Football "N" America event that featured Ruiz and Brees playing catch before the cameras. Peter Harsch, a San Diego-based prosthetist will fit Ruiz with his new leg. FNA is working to fund an additional CAF grant that will provide Ruiz with a special running leg.

Running, Saint Jude, and Danny Thomas

As part of its fundraising efforts, Saint Jude Runs are collectively one of the country's foremost athletic events for charity. Participant teams raise funds for Saint Jude Children's Research Hospital by running relay-style long distances from select cities to a Saint Jude facility. They supply their own support vehicles, such as an RV. Many friends, relatives, and businesses sponsor the challenge. There is nothing easy about the Saint Jude run or the charity itself. Both require planning, preparation, effort, resources, and faith.

In Chicago, Cardinal Mundelein created Our Lady of Guadalupe parish on the southeast side to serve the needs of a growing Mexican community in the 1920s. The Claretians traveled to Chicago to serve the parish. When Fr. James Tort became pastor of the parish, he organized the construction of the current church. Father Tort had a strong devotion to Saint Jude Thaddeus, the patron saint of hopeless causes. Night after night, as the Mexican labor force was being cut-back due to the economy, Father Tort asked Saint Jude for his intercession to help the workers of the parish. This led to the National Shrine of Saint Jude as a key part of the church.[57]

Television and movie star comedian, Danny Thomas, grew up in Toledo, Ohio. His family was Lebanese. As a child his name was Americanized from Muzyad Amos Yakhoob to Amos Jacobs. His mother was a devout Catholic and she turned her worries over to the Blessed Mother. Thomas struggled to become an entertainer—it was his vocation. He honed his craft through years of working small stages and watching others. Life's challenges continued after he got married, started a family, and moved to Detroit. In 1940, he heard a stagehand talking about how his wife had made a miraculous recovery from cancer through his prayers to Saint Jude. He started to pray to Saint Jude and promised he would "do something big" in Jude's name if he managed to gain a measure of economic security. Moving to Chicago next, his career started to build, first doing radio commercials and then club dates. He changed his name again, this time to Danny Thomas. His career took off with clean humor that played on stories with different dialects, poking fun at self-importance.

Thomas never forgot his faith, but he had pushed aside his promise to Saint Jude in his memory. He was reminded when he found a leaflet at his parish church Saint Clement about the Saint Jude novena at the National Shrine (at Our Lady of Guadalupe). Thomas moved on to New York City—top nightclubs, USO tours, movies, and finally a lead role in the long-running television comedy series, "Make Room for Daddy." He would amass funds and become a highly successful TV producer. He and his partners backed "The Andy Griffith Show" and "The Dick Van Dyke Show." Thomas's "big gift" to St. Jude was the world-famous St. Jude Children's Research Hospital in Memphis, Tennessee. He founded the institution on gifts from his fundraising efforts mostly from friends and colleagues from all faiths from the Middle East. The American Lebanese Syrian Associated Charities (ALSAC) was founded by Danny Thomas in 1957. It's the fundraising organization for Saint Jude Children's Research Hospital. From the beginning, many of those involved were giving back to a country that promised and delivered so much more than where they came. And they delivered: "No family ever receives a bill from Saint Jude for treatment, travel, housing or food—because all a family should worry about is helping their child live."[58]

ALAN SWANSON

On Wednesday, October 18, 1967, Alan Swanson and I tied for first in a cross-country race. He ran for Stony Brook of Long Island. I ran for Cheshire Academy in Connecticut. The meet was at the Choate School in Wallingford, Connecticut.

It rained hard that day. Perhaps it was fair to say that the runners were outlined against an ominous October sky.

I thought the most efficient way to run a race was to have as even a pace as possible. Many other runners were ahead of me at first. Eventually, I passed all of them.

The lead runner from Stony Brook, Alan Swanson, was surprised. He didn't know anyone was back there. He challenged me twice at the end of the race and I held him off. Finally, he tied me at the finish line.

At the social after the race, Alan and I learned that we had something else in common. We were former quarterbacks who had to give up football for cross-country.

About 20 years later, I told that story to Dean and Betty Bouzeos of the Wisconsin Fellowship of Christian Athletes. They introduced me to Jon Hanchett who worked with Native Americans in Wisconsin. He was a Stony Brook classmate of Alan Swanson.

Alan Swanson lived in Charlottesville, Virginia. He and his wife, Donna, came to the Bears' game in Washington, D.C. on November 13, 1988. The Bears beat the Redskins 34–14. I had a great time with the Swansons.

They were going to come to the Bears' game in Washington on November 26, 1989. But their son Matt had died at the age of 14. They needed to regroup. Their youngest son Allie had drawn a sketch of Matt. Their middle son Danny had written this tribute.

"Matt was the kind of boy and friend that we all needed to have. If somebody needed help, Matt would go over and help him or her. If you were feeling sad, he would come over and give you a hug. He tried as hard as he could at everything he did and usually did well despite limitations. He never tried to put anybody down, no matter how much they annoyed him. He was emotionally strong, and hardly ever cried unless he saw a friend or loved one in pain. Everyone who knew Matt loved him. If he were here right now he would probably be trying to comfort everyone that missed him. He is not alive but he will live on in our memories."

Danny cited Mark 10:16 which reads, *"And he took the children in his arms, put his hands on them and blessed them."*

My wife and our children and I were invited to the Swansons for a visit. We celebrated our anniversary on Saturday, March 3. Then we started our drive there on Sunday. We arrived on Monday. We stayed until Thursday morning.

During our visit, we learned that Alan and Donna met while they were students at Furman University. When he was a sophomore, his father called with the news that the family business, Thomas English Muffins, had been sold.

Alan's share enabled him to do what he wanted to do for a living. He chose to teach seventh grade. I sat in on his English class and learned how to have fun with commas. He let me teach his history classes. We showed the video, "George Halas and the Chicago Bears." Then we talked about the history of the team and the National Football League. We also felt compelled to talk about the cross-country race where Alan tied me for first.

Alan later told me that he hopes the McCaskeys never sell the Bears. He said, *"It's the only time you'll really do something together as a family."*

My wife, Gretchen, and I visited Thomas Jefferson's house, Monticello, because she used to play the cello. We visited the Swansons when the Bears played the Redskins in Washington on December 9, 1990. The Swansons moved to another house because there were so many memories of Matt where they had lived. I was their basketball hoop consultant.

Many years later, Alan coached baseball at Saint Anne's-Belfield School in Charlottesville. He won five state baseball championships, including two with Kyle Long.

One time Alan went out to the mound to take Kyle out of a game. Kyle refused to leave. Alan went back to the dugout and said to the pitching coach, *"If you want him out of the game, you go out there and get him."*

In 2013, I made a literary pilgrimage to Earl Hamner's hometown of Schuyler, Virginia. It's about thirty miles south of Charlottesville. There is a museum and visitors can walk through his childhood home. Before I went there, I had break-fast with Alan. He told me that the Bears should draft Kyle Long, which we did.

John Johnson Works for the Good of All

John Johnson found success on the football field in high school, college, and the pros. At Hobart High School, he played for In-diana Hall-of-Fame Coach Russ Deal on the 1957-1959 winning football teams that posted a record of 24-2-1. The "Brickies" were undefeated in 1959. That year, Johnson was named to the All-State Football Team and the High School All-American Team.

At Indiana University, Johnson played for Coach Phil Dickens. Johnson was named All-Big Ten in 1962 and select-ed to play in the 1962 Blue-Gray Football Christmas Classic and the Crusade Bowl for Cancer. The 1963 Indiana Univer-sity graduate is a member of the Indiana Hall of Fame.

Johnson was a sixth round draft choice of the Chicago Bears in 1963 and he played for Head Coach George Halas. Before his pro career, he had played on the offensive line, but was converted to a defensive tackle for the Bears. Johnson played for the talented 1963 World Champions that beat the

New York Giants, 14-10, for the NFL's top prize. The Bears posted a season record of 11-1-2 and the team would be known as one of the Bears' best in history. Like today, every player on the squad was important for the success of the team and Johnson replaced an injured Fred Williams in the Championship game and had 9 tackles.[59]

Once Johnson left football, he had a successful business career as the chairman, owner, and managing director of the John Joseph Group. He has led substantial efforts for charities serving on the board of directors for several—raising money for the Brian Piccolo Cancer Research Fund, NFL Alumni Chicago Chapter, "Caring for Kids," Maryville home for children, Misericordia, and Better Boys Foundation. Johnson is a member of the Sports Faith International Hall of Fame.

If and When

I present a rewrite of Rudyard Kipling's "If" poem. My poem is "When." Like the original there are eleven syllables in a line, then ten, eleven then ten, throughout the poem.

When

When you strive and thrive for excellence rather
Than rationalize mediocrity
And can realize that you are no better than
Anyone else but certainly no worse,
When you know the sun will appear after an
Eclipse and know that apathy is the

Opposite of love and not hate, and not be
Self-centered so you listen to others,

When you can dream positively and think
Actively so that you can assist friends
Rather than handicap them and be grateful
To the good God for your natural gifts,
When you can have people take your earnestly
Through a feeling of duty and a sense
Of humor and yet be unique and make your
Presence felt without being obnoxious,

When you maintain a belief in love and
Laughter rather than loneliness and tears,
When you stand in love rather than fall in it
And choose love gladly rather than madly,
When you need someone because you love her
Rather than love someone since you need her
When you have double cartwheels with only her
And have universal brotherly love,

When foes goad you into prudence rather than
Stupefy you into resignation,
When you are strong with faith in humanity
Rather than aggressive from fear of it,
When you maintain a belief in the last
Flower and the wild flag and also play
The trumpet of the swan to catch the white deer,
Then you will be BAM: becoming a man.

IRVING BERLIN

GOD BLESS AMERICA, IRVING BERLIN

Irving Berlin was born May 11, 1888, in Russia. In 1893, he moved with his family to New York City. At the age of eight, he sang songs while he sold newspapers. At the age of thirteen, he sang to saloon customers. At the age of eighteen, he was a singing waiter. He sang parodies of the hit songs. He taught himself to play piano. At the age of twenty, he became a songwriter.

In 1912, he married Dorothy Goetz. They honeymooned in Havana. She died six months later of typhoid fever.

In 1917, he was drafted into the Army. One newspaper headline was "Army takes Berlin." He wrote a revue which included a song that he also performed, "Oh! How I Hate to Get Up in the Morning."

In 1918, he was on a train and sang to the passengers. They asked him how he knew so many songs. He replied, *"I wrote them."*

In 1925, he fell in love with Ellin Mackay.[60] He wooed her with the writing of the song "Always." They were married for 63 years until she died in 1988.

In 1938, he gave a song that he had written 20 years earlier, "God Bless America," to Kate Smith. All of the royalties from "God Bless America" have been donated to the Boy Scouts and the Girl Scouts. He learned the phrase "God bless America" from his mother.

In 1942, Berlin wrote the song "White Christmas" for Bing Crosby in the movie "Holiday Inn." Berlin won an Academy Award for it.

He wrote a stage show, "This is the Army." It was shown at military bases all over the world. He traveled with it for 3 1/2 years and sang "Oh! How I Hate to Get Up in the Morning." He donated all of the profits to the Army.

In 1946, Jerome Kern was working on "Annie Get Your Gun" until he died. Richard Rodgers and Oscar Hammerstein II persuaded Berlin to replace Kern. The show had many songs including "You Can't Get A Man With A Gun," and "Anything

You Can Do, I Can Do Better." Ethel Merman made Berlin's song "There's No Business Like Show Business" her trademark.

Berlin did not believe in inspiration. He believed in work. He wrote 1,500 songs including "Easter Parade." At the age of 101, he died in his sleep on September 22, 1989, in New York City.

PULLMAN CENTER WALL-RAISING

On September 17, 1920, the original meeting for what is now the National Football League took place at Ralph Hay's Hupmobile Showroom in Canton, Ohio. That's why the Pro Football Hall of Fame is located there. There weren't enough chairs for Hay and Halas and the other founding fathers. So, they sat on the fenders and the running boards of the cars.

From this humble beginning, the NFL has grown so much that it is able to make a grant to the Pullman Community Center.

There are many things about which we can worry and even more about which we should be grateful. God has been very, very good to us. It's amazing how many people are helping to build the Pullman Community Center. We promise to be good stewards of our finances and our resources and our blessings. There is much about which we can fret. Better yet to thank God for all things.

The Chicago Bears were thrilled to celebrate the wall-raising of the Pullman Community Center on May 2, 2018. This facility will serve as a tremendous resource for deserving families and children in neighborhoods throughout this area. We are particularly encouraged by the numerous new athletic and fitness opportunities that will be available. Our organization has a long history of promoting health and fitness, and we are excited to expand our investment in Chicago's children by supporting this wonderful new facility.

We know that athletics pay dividends in the lives of young people, their healthy development and the unity and vibrancy of their communities. We hope the athletic fields in this facility will serve not only as a great home for spirited athletic competition, but for community events and family activities in the years ahead.[61]

Like football itself, this project is a true team effort, and it would not be possible without the dedication, vision, and support of many businesses and community leaders.

Let the Pullman Community Center be a reminder: God performs miracles for people of faith who diligently work together.

JAMES CAMERON AND FRANK FAUNCE

Cliff Stein is a Senior Vice President and In House Counsel for the Chicago Bears. After I had surgery for prostate cancer, he gave me a book of stories about overcoming adversity. The book is *Supersurvivors: The Surprising Link Between Suffering and Success* by David Feldman and Lee Kravetz. The most compelling story to me was about James Cameron. He grew up in Marion, Indiana.

In August 1930, when Cameron was 16 years old, he had gone out with two older teenage African-American friends, Thomas Shipp and Abram Smith. They attempted to rob a young white man, Claude Deeter, and his girlfriend, Mary Ball, who were in a parked car. Cameron had been pressured by one of his older friends to be the stickup man. When Cameron approached the vehicle and opened the door, he and Deeter recognized each other. Cameron dropped the gun and ran away before one of the other boys shot Deeter in the robbery confrontation. Deeter died in the hospital. The three youths were quickly arrested, and on the same night charged with robbery, murder, and rape. (The rape charge was later dropped.)

A mob broke into the jail where Cameron and his two friends were being held. The mob at the Grant County Courthouse square took all three youths from the jail. Ship was taken out and beaten, and hanged from the bars of his jail window; Smith was dead from the beating before the mob hanged both boys from a tree in the square.

Cameron was beaten and a noose was put around his neck. Cameron remembered hearing the voice of an unidentified woman saying that he was not guilty. Cameron was led back to the jail.

At trial, Cameron was represented by two African American attorneys who convinced jurors of his innocence of charges that might have led to a life sentence. Cameron was convicted as being an accessory to the crime of voluntary manslaughter. He served four years at an Indiana State Reformatory.[62]

After he was paroled, he moved to Detroit, Michigan, where he worked at Stroh Brewery Company and attended Wayne State University."

Cameron became a boiler engineer and a civil rights activist. According to Feldman and Kravetz, "He felt that God had a mission for him: to turn his suffering, guilt, and anger into something precious—a way of making the world a better place." The murder of Deeter and the lynching of Ship and Smith affected many families in Marion. Cameron himself wrote and spoke about it extensively. Several voices have been heard over the years.[63]

FRANK FAUNCE

In his essay "The United States of Lyncherdom," Mark Twain wrote, "no mob has any sand in the presence of a man known to be splendidly brave…When I was a boy I saw a brave gentleman deride and insult a mob and drive it away."

Retired U.S. Army Colonel Frank Faunce has conveyed his father's story about the lynching in Marion. His father, also named Frank, was an All American halfback at Indiana University. During World War II, he became an aeronautical engineer at the Wright Patterson Army Air Corps Research Center and later worked for Grumman Aircraft. In retirement, he also did some notable archeological work in Florida.

Faunce's story recently came to the attention of Jeff Keag and Brad Cook at Indiana University and my publisher, Larry Norris. Here is what Retired Colonel Faunce provided:

"When my twin brother Albert and I were about ten years old (60+ years ago), our father told us the story of his saving James Cameron's life…while he was removing the noose from James Cameron's neck, my aunt Mary screamed my father's name because she was concerned about his safety. He told the story as an object lesson about not being part of a mob...well known among our family and friends, but nobody ever talked to us until now.

"The story my father told Albert and me was that he and sister Mary drove down to the Courthouse Square to see what was going on and they parked my grandfather's model T Ford automobile on a side street and walked over to an ice cream parlor on the square where he left his sister while he went over to the county jail which was a block away on the other side of the square. He said when he got to the jail there was a mob of about 50 or 60 people who were trying to take the three boys...He told us that as he tried to reason with some of the men in the mob, someone came up behind him and hit him in the head and knocked him unconscious on the steps leading to the Sheriff's house and jail.

"He said when he regained consciousness, he heard the riot over by the courthouse and ran over just in time to see a man putting a noose around James Cameron's neck. He said he jumped up and pushed the man out of the way and lifted the noose from James Cameron's neck, he yelled to the mob, 'You're not going to hang this boy!' James Cameron was shaking and my father put his arm around the youngster's shoulders to steady him and he walked the 16-year old boy through the stunned crowd back to the jail where he turned him over to the police."

Frank Faunce was an All American football halfback and athlete at Indiana University. His son Albert played football at Northwestern during the Ara Parseghian era. His grandson Jay played for Indiana University. "

FAMILY THAT PRAYS TOGETHER STAYS TOGETHER

Pope Francis advanced the sainthood cause of Holy Cross Father Patrick Peyton. The Pope approved the decree recognizing his heroic virtues on December 18, 2017, with Cardinal Angelo Amato, Prefect of the Congregation for Saints' Causes. Now, a miracle is needed for his beatification and a second one for his canonization.

Father Peyton had wanted to become a priest, but his applications to seminaries had been rejected back in Ireland. He emigrated from Ireland to the United States in 1928 with the intention to seek business success. But soon afterward, he found himself recommitted to the priesthood. He and his brother Tom worked as janitors at the Cathedral of Saint Peter in Scranton, Pennsylvania. Holy Cross priests from Notre Dame, Indiana, visited Scranton. The Peytons decided to join the Holy Cross Order. While in the seminary, Patrick became gravely ill with tuberculosis. He turned to the Blessed Mother and prayed the rosary as he had done with his parents back in Ireland. His lungs cleared and he continued with his schooling. He and his brother were ordained priests with the Congregation of the Holy Cross in 1941.

His mission became clear in 1942, with the world racked by war and the pending crisis in the family looming. He said he was "given" a message of family prayer and the praying of the Rosary. The success of his undertaking was phenomenal.[64]

The "Rosary Priest" pioneered Catholic media in the 1940s on the radio and then television. To get things started, Father

Peyton tried to sell a New York radio station on a Catholic program, but was told he needed celebrity support. After nervously calling Bing Crosby and convincing him to back his efforts, his first radio show was broadcast on May 13, 1945. It featured Archbishop Spellman of New York and President Harry Truman.

Stars such as Grace Kelly, Gregory Peck, Rosalind Russell, Jimmy Stewart, Ronald Reagan, James Dean, Bob Newhart, Jack Benny, Loretta Young, and Frank Sinatra worked with Father Peyton. He founded Holy Cross Family Ministries, which includes Family Rosary, Family Theater Productions, Father Peyton Family Institute, and Family Rosary International. Father Peyton's ministry produced over 10,000 broadcasts. He also conducted rosary crusades for millions. "The family that prays together stays together" was his motto.[65] Fr Peyton died in 1992.

DIFFERENT TESTS

As a 5-10 eighth grader,
I had to choose
Between basketball and speed-skating.
Basketball had cheerleaders.
After high school and only three more inches,
I had to give up football
Because of eye problems.
So I ran cross-country.

After two seasons,
I had to give up cross-country
Because of allergy problems.
So I wrote humor,
I became immune to many allergies,
But not kryptonite.
So I started running again.
My test was easier than Job's.
His was essay.
Mine was multiple choice.

UNDER PRESSURE

It's not easy being an ideal husband. I'm under a lot of pressure. There are no days off. My wife and her mother wanted me to encourage other husbands to do as much as I do around the house. If I did anymore around the house, I'd have lost my self-respect.

There is a division of labor in our home. I am the dishwasher, the garbage man, and the laundry man. As dishwasher, I feel that I do not deserve another meal until I have cleaned up the dishes from the previous one. My wife is the cleaning lady, the cook, and the shopper. When we do our chores together, we are like Torvill and Dean.[66]

I have lost some weight. I hope that I am not anorexic. Just in case, I have signed my will. As far as I know, all of my apologies and thank yous are up-to-date. It has been a wonderful life, starring Jimmy Stewart and Donna Reed. Please take care of my wife; she has been an answered prayer. If you ever need a colostomy, she can teach you how to take care of it.

My wife and I are enjoying married life. After we say good night, she doesn't have to drive home. She is already there. She has signed her will. I get everything.

When I was on my honeymoon, with my wife, after I had told a joke, I quoted Jimmy Durante. I said, *"I got a million of them."*

She replied, *"I wish you only had a thousand."*

On Easter Sunday, 1984, I said, *"I have chest pains."*

My wife replied, *"Not now, I'm cross-stitching."*

In November of 1985, I had to survive the flu because the Chicago gravediggers were on strike.

Christmas is very demanding in our home. First my wife wants a tree. Next she wants a gift. Then she expects me to be cheerful.

I once thought that my wife was a lot like my mother. My wife worked and worked and worked and never complained. Then she complained.

My wife liked to have our sons watch me do my chores. I hoped that they would go to the dentist on a regular basis. She hoped that they turned in their term papers on time. I have the best teeth in the family.

Saint Brendan of Birr

Saint Brendan of Birr is one of the twelve apostles of Ireland, Irish monastic saints of the 6th century who studied under Saint Finnian at Clonard Abbey. Saint Brendan was born about 500 AD and many think he died about 572. Sometimes this saint is confused with another Irish Monastic Saint, St Brendan of Clonfert (the Navigator). Saint Brendan of Birr became friends of St Columba (also known as Columbkille) and St Brendan the Navigator. It was at this time the monks of Ireland began a period of 300 years of manuscript copying and creation. The Book of Kells being the most famous illuminated manuscript is said to come from one of the monasteries of Saint Columba—the Kells Monastery or perhaps created at Iona in whole or in part and then shipped to Kells for safety.

Saint Brendan of Birr founded a monastery at Birr in central Ireland although everything we know about Brendan comes from the writings on other Irish Saints.

Saint Brendan worked for the "good of the league." After some accusations were made about Saint Columba, he faced excommunication. Saint Brendan defended him and told others that Columba was held in high esteem by God. Saint Brendan's defense allowed Saint Columba to continue and he would go on to found his celebrated monastery at Iona, an island in the Inner Hebrides off the coast of Scotland.

Saint Brendan of Birr's feast day is November 29th. Brendan's monastery at Birr is said by some to have created the MacRegol Gospels (after Brendan's death), which are now housed at the Bodleian Library in Oxford.

QUIZ—ANYTHING GOES

Walter Payton was always clowning around at Halas Hall. Skilled at impersonation, one day the phone rang and in his best Pat McCaskey voice he said, "Let me answer the phone. Give me something to do." Another time when my father's phone rang, he picked it up and said, "This is Bernice. Mister McCaskey can't come to the phone right now because I'm giving him a full body massage." Around Halas Hall, Payton used to say "all the McCaskeys look alike." He liked to joke around the office, but on both the practice and playing field, he was a fierce competitor.

Here are questions that I think Walter would have appreciated.

Questions

1. When I met this player's father the night before Super Bowl XX, I said to him, "You should have given [him] more spankings." His response was, "I know." Who was the player?
2. We had a run to start off training camp and I used to take part and did quite well. In 1981, Kris Haines finished ahead of me. What happened to him?
3. Which seldom-seen character from the Mary Tyler More show had the catchphrase "A little song, a little dance, a little seltzer down your pants?"
4. Referring to Greek history, what did Frank Shorter ask at the 20-mile mark of his first marathon?
5. Which famous Bears fan, comedian, and actor often included talk of his fondness for the team and his dislike of the Packers on his TV Show "
6. In the original Brian's Song movie from 1971, who played Gale Sayers?
7. In the original Brian's Song movie from 1971, who played Brian Piccolo?
8. In the original Brian's Song movie from 1971, who played George Halas?
9. Who became a star on the "Donna Reed Show" and singer of "Johnny Angel?" This actress played Joy Piccolo in "Brian's Song."
10. The Super Bowl Shuffle reached the Billboard Top 100 and was nominated for what?

Answers:

1. I was talking to Jim McMahon's dad, also named Jim McMahon.
2. Kris Haines was cut.
3. Chuckles the Clown—the MTM show about Chuckles's funeral is considered by many to be one of the funniest shows of all time.
4. Frank Shorter said, "Why couldn't Pheidippides have died here?" Pheidippides was the original Greek soldier who ran from Marathon to Athens (about 26 miles) to announce the Greeks' victory over the Persians and then he died.[67]
5. Jim Belushi.
6. Billy Dee Williams.
7. James Caan.
8. Jack Warden.
9. Shelley Fabares.
10. A Grammy.

PATRICK MCCASKEY

WIN CHAMPIONSHIPS WITH SPORTSMANSHIP.

INTRODUCTION

Brian Urlacher and Walter Payton both spent their entire careers with the Chicago Bears. We are glad they did. Both were exemplary athletes—both were take-no-prisoner competitors, but they played clean.

Urlacher was a 6-foot-4, 260 pound middle linebacker who was so freaky quick and fast that he could cover receivers like a defensive back. The word "mismatch" was not used when Urlacher was patrolling his position. And as hard as Urlacher could tackle, opponents knew he was not taking aim to do them harm; he was always aiming to play the game well. Urlacher was also a positive team player who was there for his teammates when they needed his help.

Walter Payton could do anything in football, anything! But a beautiful part of Payton's game was his constant enthusiasm, energy, and sportsmanship. Payton was the running back who refused to go down. He came at defenders with more thrust than a rocket. He blocked for his teammates and no job was beneath him—in fact he was always wanting to do more. And when he was tackled, he often sprung up from the pile and paid respect to the players who had tackled him.[68]

Both Payton and Urlacher demonstrated the way the Bears want to win Championships. Both have been inducted in the Pro Football Hall of Fame. We do not want to win with dirty tricks and gimmicks. We want to win by playing fair and with good character, showing respect and exhibiting virtue. So this commandment means ***succeed with good character.***

GENE PINGATORE

Gene Pingatore is the long-time Head Basketball Coach at Saint Joseph High School in Westchester, Illinois. The 1000-game winner was inducted into the Sports Faith International Hall of Fame, which calls attention to the accomplishments of exemplary athletes, coaches, and teams. Pingatore's program focuses on character and discipline. Pingatore uses a consistent approach to help his young men. Once the Saint Joseph's program was feeding players into NCAA Division 1 Colleges on scholarships, players from all over the area started coming to the high school.[69]

Pingatore attended Saint Mel High School on Chicago's west side and then went on to play basketball at Loyola Marymount. After graduation, he returned to Chicago to do graduate work at Loyola University and DePaul University. In 1960, he began a coaching and teaching career at the newly built Saint Joseph High School in Westchester, Illinois. He was the assistant coach for 9 years. Then he became the head coach. He has served in many capacities at the school and is currently in his 49th year as head basketball coach.

With over 1,000 victories, he gives the credit to his coaches and to his players. I have seen him coach; he is well behaved and he is well dressed. He is not an "in your face" coach; he is a gentleman and he is a teacher.

Pingatore and his Saint Joe's program is the standard-bearer of excellence in High School basketball. According to the Saint Joe's web site, his list of accomplishments are as follows: Gene Pingatore captured 27 East Suburban Catholic Conference Championships, 2 Catholic League North titles, 9 prestigious Proviso West Holiday Tournament Championships, 34 state regional titles and 13 state sectional titles. In 1978, 1982, 1983, 1984, 1986, 1987, and 1999, his teams qualified for the Elite Eight Tournament. In 2015 his team qualified for the Final Four in Peoria and won the 3A Illinois State Title. The 1978 team was the state runner-up; the 1984 team placed 4th; the 1987 team took 3rd place; and the 1999 team captured the Class AA Illinois State Championship. In 2016, Saint Joseph returned to the 3A Final Four and placed 4th in State.

Gene Pingatore coached more than a dozen fine players who went on to the pros. Perhaps his most well-known former basketball player is Isaiah Thomas. Pingatore's basketball alums also include two NFL players as well: Andy Frederick and Cameron Meredith.

Gene Pingatore has received dozens of coaching honors and many awards honoring his character and leadership. He has worked on many boards and organizations that serve the community and youth.

BILL WENNINGTON

Bill Wennington is a 7-foot tall 245 pound former professional basketball player who won several championships during his long career. "Wennington's story is one of great patience, hard work, and a burning desire to succeed."[70]

Wennington was adopted; his mom told him from an early age that he was chosen. In sports, he received encouragement early on from his high school coach, Bob McKillopp.

Faith has always been a part of his life—faith that allows him to be a whole person, helps drive him to be his best, and gives him something to believe in that is greater than himself. Wennington says that faith doesn't make everything easy, but it can make you better.

Wennington played basketball for New York's Long Island Lutheran Middle and High School, Saint John's University, the Dallas Mavericks, the Sacramento Kings, Virtus Bologna in Italy, and the Chicago Bulls. He played for 11 seasons in the NBA. Chicago teammates included Steve Kerr, Ron Harper, Michael Jordan, Scottie Pippen and Dennis Rodman.

As a high school player, he led his team to two state titles. At Saint John's University, the broadcasting major played in the NCAA Men's Final Four as a member of the 1985 Redmen.

After his early years with the NBA Mavericks and Kings, his career stalled and he signed with Virtus Bologna in Italy. He did it with the support of his wife, Ann, although she was 7 months pregnant. Wennington earned one championship ring from Virtus Bologna and an MVP in the playoffs. His fine performance in Italy led to his signing with Bulls and the opportunity to play on one of the greatest teams in NBA history.

Wennington has three championship rings from the Chicago Bulls. He retired as a player after the 1999-2000 NBA season. Today, the former Canadian Olympian and McDonald's All-American is a broadcaster for the Bulls.

Sports and Faith Series readers may remember that the author is a big fan of the Chip Hilton Sports books. In Volume Two, *Championship Ball*, Taps Browning moved next door to Chip Hilton. Then they were teammates at Valley Falls High School.

In 1993, Wennington, his wife, Ann, and their son, Rob, moved next door to me, my wife, Gretchen, and our sons, Ed, Tom, and Jim. Jim and Rob were classmates at Saint Mary's School, Loyola Academy, and Boston College.

Wennington has been inducted into the Quebec Basketball Hall of Fame and the Canadian Basketball Hall of Fame. He was also inducted into the Sports Faith International Hall of Fame in 2016.

IC Catholic Prep Football Team

When I was a Notre Dame High School senior, my prom date was a cheerleader for Immaculate Conception High School. The school is now known as IC Catholic Prep (ICCP). The school is not in the witness protection program. It simply has a different name. I had nothing to do with it.

The 2016 IC Catholic Prep football team was 14–0, winning the Class 3A State of Illinois Championship.

The team does three service projects a year: The Knights of Columbus Fish Fry, Touchdowns for Cancer through Saint Jude, and the Drew Fest which raises awareness and money for eosinophilic esophagitis.

Tom Schergen is the athletic director at IC Catholic Prep. Bill Krefft is the head football coach. Both men have been teaching special education.

Coach Krefft was a player on the 2002 IC Catholic Prep State Championship team. He was an assistant coach on the 2008 IC Catholic Prep State Championship team. He was the head coach on the 2016 IC Catholic Prep State Championship team. Sports Faith International honored the IC Catholic Prep football team by inducting them into the SFI Hall of Fame.

Double Stuff

The Knights won a second straight state championship in 2017 with a convincing 35–0 win over Pleasant Plains at Northern Illinois University's Huskie Stadium. It was IC Catholic Prep's fourth title overall and second consecutive.

John Byner and John Wayne

March 23, 2017

On December 1
My grandson was born.
Please hold the sarcasm;
There's another Pat McCaskey
In the world.

On January 23,
I had surgery
To remove a growth
From my inner ear.
It was an opportunity
To do John Byner's impersonation
Of John Wayne as a brain surgeon.
"We're gonna have ta yank it out of there."

Before the surgery,
Father Nacius had anointed me.
My ear is healed.

And here's John Byner's impersonation
of John Wayne as a priest.
"Well, dominus vobiscum."

UNIVERSITY OF SAINT FRANCIS FOOTBALL TEAM

Sports Faith International honored the 2016 University of
Saint Francis Cougars football team from Fort Wayne, Indiana, by inducting then into the SFI Hall of Fame. The team
won the NAIA Championship. Offseason, they traveled to El
Salvador to build homes for the homeless.

On December 16, 2016, Saint Francis won the championship game, beating Baker University of Kanas, 38–17. Offensive player of the game, Seth Coate, had 9 receptions for
180 yards and 3 touchdowns. Lucas Sparks had 6 tackles,

including 2.5 tackles for loss and 1.5 sacks. He also forced and recovered a fumble. He was the defensive player of the game. Mike McCaffrey is the athletic director. Kevin Donley was the NAIA Coach of the Year.

TWO FOR THE COUGARS

The Cougars finished the 2017 season with a second-straight NAIA national title. It wasn't easy. In the first game of the playoffs, the Cougars struggled against Benedictine College of Atchison, Kansas. On a stormy night, the Cougars came from behind to win, 26–21, after the Ravens led, 14–6, at the half.

On Saturday night, December 16, 2017, Saint Francis University beat Reinhardt University of Waleska, Georgia, 24–13, in the NAIA Championship game in Daytona Beach. The Cougars finished the season at 14–0. Nick Ferrer, NAIA Player of the Year, had 270 yards passing and Duke Blackwell had 4 receptions for 96 yards for the Cougars. Ferrer finished his college career with 136 touchdown passes, the second most in NAIA history. Running back Justin Green ran for 132 yards and 2 touchdowns. Linebacker, Eric Dunten, recorded 17 tackles to lead the way on defense.

1961 DONS

When I was a junior at Notre Dame High School in the fall of 1965, Larry Raymond's sister, Louise, was my date for the homecoming dance. Larry drove us. We double dated so that we would be safe. He told us about the 1961 football team that won every game.

From Larry and the yearbook, we know:

"A few of the outstanding names on this year's squad were Greg Schilling, the break-away halfback, Al Loboy, the shoulder-dipping fullback, and Tom Francisco, the team's brick wall situated at guard. A completely successful season cannot be attributed to just several individuals, because it was always a team effort.

"Led by junior quarterback Rick Gorzynski, the Dons defeated Taft, 14–13. The next week Notre Dame hit the road to Wheaton where Saint Francis was downed, 27–0. Coming home for the next game, Al Loboy and Jim Prasch sparked the Dons in their 34–0 victory over Saint Bede.

"Suburban Catholic Conference play opened with a triumph over Saint Procopius, 33–6. Greg Schilling's four touchdowns helped make him the only junior on the Suburban All-Star team. At Marmion, on a recovered fumble by Larry Raymond, the Dons won, 12–6. In the next three conference games, Notre Dame held their opponents to seven points, the Dons scored 96. Patterson, Francisco, Buonicontro, and Gibbons led the defense in the defeat of I.C. (Immaculate Conception), 27–0; J.C. (Joliet Catholic), 27–7; and Saint Ed's, 42–0.

"The Dons went downstate to run over Peoria Spaulding, which was the number four team in the state, 21–0, on touchdowns by Loboy and Schilling. The crowning touch for Coach Yonto came in Woodstock where Notre Dame sank Marian, 46–28."

1966 DONS

If the Apostles had played football, they would have been a great team like the 1966 Dons. Jesus would have been the coach like Bill Casey, Jack Cole, Denny Conway, Al Loboy, and Fran Willett.

Peter would have been the quarterback, like Bill Harrington, Roy Vana, Tom Lange, and me. Andrew was Peter's brother. They would have been used to playing catch in the yard. Let's put Andrew at end like John Clausen, Bob Dorsch, John Ellefson, Jim Lannon, Ken Powers, and Frank Urban.

James the son of Zebedee and his brother, John, were known as the sons of thunder. They would have been the backs like Gary Aylesworth, Owen Bauler, Charlie Bilodeau, Tom Bunzol, Bob Feltz, Dan Governile, Mark Havlis, Kevin Host, Pat Hughes, Gary Keating, Gary Lund, Greg Luzinski, Mike Newton, Tom Newton, and Kevin Saint James.

We don't know much about Philip, Bartholomew, James the son of Alphaeus, Thaddeus, and Simon the Canaanean. So they would have been the lineman like Bob Allen, Larry Amidei, Gerry Bannon, Bob Blaney, John Debbout, Mike Hughes, Jerry Jasinski, Brian Kelly, Jim King, Bill Marquardt, Pete Newell, John Nadolski, Glenn O'Grady, Bob Rammon,

Rick Rammon, Mike Rolnicki, Dick Ryglowski, Mike Shaw, Rich Simko, Greg Szymanski, Jim Weides, Bob Zientara, Tom Zizak, and Sam Zuccaro.

Doubting Thomas would always be encouraging his teammates to play harder. Let's put him at linebacker like Mike Fragale, Tom Kusmerz, Greg Luzinski, Kevin Murning-han, Tom Newton, Joe Petricca, Ken Powers, Bruce Scacco, and me. If Ken Powers had been an apostle, the other apostles wouldn't have slept in the Garden of Gethsemane.

Matthew the tax collector had great attention to detail. Let's put him at manager like Marty Peterson and Marty Ward.

Matthias, who replaced Judas, would have been the kicker like Steve Hurley.

Paul would have been the writer like Ken Kubiesa, John McCarthy, John O'Connor, and me. Paul wrote a lot of letters even though the Corinthians were the only ones who ever wrote back.

1966 Junior Senior Game

The 1966 Notre Dame High School varsity football team was 9–0 and outscored opponents 341–80. After the season, on Friday, November 18, the seniors and the freshmen played the juniors and the sophomores.

Fullback Greg Luzinski had been the only junior to start every game on offense. Left outside linebacker Joe Petricca had been the only junior to start every game on defense. They played with the juniors and the sophomores.

Ken Powers played fullback for the seniors and the freshmen. Freshman Gary Potempa played left outside linebacker for the seniors and the freshmen.

Right before the kickoff Coach Willett said to me, *"You can pass as much as you want."*

I thought, *"I'll show him. We'll run it every play."*

To start the game, Steve Hurley kicked off to the juniors and the sophomores. On their first possession, Luzinski had a touchdown run. Then he kicked the extra point.

I got angry. I hollered at my teammates in the huddle to take the game seriously or we wouldn't win. Center Mike Shaw had an interesting rebuttal. He said, *"Don't worry about it. We're going to win."*

I apologized to them and then called wedge blocking over right guard Bill Marquardt. Right halfback Mike Newton and Powers took turns carrying the ball. When Marquardt needed a break, I called wedge blocking over left guard Dick Ryglowski.

In many huddles, Powers told the offensive linemen that the blocking was great. Left tackle Pete Newell was grateful for the recognition.

In the first quarter, Powers had a touchdown run. Hurley kicked the extra point.

In the second quarter, Powers had a touchdown run. Hurley kicked the extra point.

In the third quarter, I called belly option eight. I faked to Powers off right tackle Jerry Jasinski, and kept it around right end Pat Hughes for a touchdown. Hurley kicked the extra point.

In the fourth quarter, there were many substitutions. The coaches did not sing "Send in the Clowns." The seniors and the freshmen won 21–7.

Saint Dominic de Guzman

Many of our civil and religious leaders come from prominent families. Dominic was born in the year 1170 at Calaruega, Castile, Spain, of a noble family. His father was royal warden of the village and his mother was to become Blessed Joan of Aza. Dominic was born to serve God through the Church. He and his two brothers would become priests. He founded the Order of Preachers, the Dominicans. Dominic is called the "light of the Church."

Conflict in the Church has been around since its beginning. During Dominic's time, there were substantial threats from heresy. All the good that has come about in the creation of the Dominicans as the Order of Preachers is based on what was needed at the time.

As a young man, Dominic was known for his piety. The Bishop of Osma made him a Canon Regular of his church. Diego de Acebo, the Prior of the community saw that Dominic learned the basics of religious life and contemplation. Diego became bishop of Osma and invited Dominic to travel with him on a diplomatic mission.[71]

At the age of 25, Dominic was ordained. Traveling in France, he passed through an area where the Albigensian heresy was winning supporters. A brief successful encounter with one person who had fallen away convinced Dominic that he should be teaching. Dominic joined up with monks from Saint Bernard's monastery on a mission to convert the Albigensians.

Albigensians, also called the Cathars, believed in dualism of two opposing principles, good and evil. All matter regarded as evil led to the conclusion that the creator of the material world was a devil. Dominic and others worked diligently to correct this error. Dominic established a community in Prouille, which served as a shelter for women converted from heresy and a kind of basecamp for him. This humble beginning was the

FATHER LAWRENCE LEW AT SAINT DOMINIC'S BIRTHPLACE

seed that grew all the communities of Dominican Sisters.[72] As the Dominican Priests and Brothers set out on their missions, cloistered Dominican Nuns supported them in prayer. Dominican Sisters established themselves in preaching through teaching and many other activities.

Truth is a motto of the Dominicans. Dominic set out to persuade the Cathars of their errors, but in 1208, after the murder of a papal legate by the Cathars, Pope Innocent III called on a crusade to suppress the heresy by force of arms. Dominic continued his peaceful ways of persuasion, but Catholic forces led by Simon de Montfort battled the Albigensian forces led by the Count of Toulouse. Montfort was victorious but in his wake was left destruction and death. Dominic would follow the battles and help the survivors and pray for the combatants. With each stop on his journey, Dominic was more aware of the devastation that was born out of ignorance. The Order of Preachers could help.

There was an Inquisition in the 12th century that was carried out by a group of institutions within the Catholic Church combatting heresy. Although this early Inquisition gave some discipline to the quelling of heresies and added legal process; it could also lead to brutal punishments that were carried out by civil authorities. In the 12th century the problem of heresy had become more troubling as it was spreading fast with large groups.

Dominic set out to create a new religious order whose members led lives of contemplation and prayer. His men would pray, meditate, and train in theology—practice perpetual abstinence from meat, live in poverty, and depend upon alms for subsistence. They would be directed from a central authority. They would be expert and zealous preachers. They would go out like the Apostles to the corners of the world and preach the gospel. Their discipline and devotion would help them succeed where others had failed.

Dominic was devoted to the Rosary and he prayed the rosary as the church battled the heresy. Today, the Dominicans promote the Rosary as a *"spiritual weapon to fight a cultural battle for life, family, and a just society."*[73] Without study, prayer, and meditation, Dominic's preachers have nothing to offer. The second Dominican motto is "to contemplate and to give to others the fruits of contemplation."

In 1214, Dominic went to Rome to attend the Fourth Lateran Council. Pope Innocent III approved the community at Prouille, but formal approval of Dominic's order took a few more years. After Pope Innocent died, Pope Honorius III was elected and he formally confirmed Dominic's order and its constitutions in December of 1216. His order lived under the rule of Saint Augustine.[74]

Dominic formed friendships with Cardinal Ugolino (the future Gregory IX) and Francis of Assisi. The founders of the Order of Preachers and the Franciscans were different people, but both were determined to send their members out into the world to save it. Dominic continued to establish new monasteries in locations that are known today as part of Italy, Spain, and France. He was also asked by the Pope to create one community of nuns in Rome to replace many scattered and unorganized homes. Most communities were begun at Universities.

The Dominicans would become the voice of scholastic theology and philosophy. The Dominicans spread to Poland, Scandinavia, and Palestine. Dominic's successors went to the cities of Canterbury, London, and Oxford.

Dominic fell ill and journeyed to a Dominican monastery in Bologna where he died August 6, 1221. In 1234, Pope Gregory IX signed the decree of canonization. Saint Dominic is the patron saint of Astronomers and the Dominican Republic. His "coaching tree" includes Dominican "giants" such as Saint Albert the Great, Saint Thomas Aquinas, and Saint Catherine of Siena.[75]

HOWARD COSELL

QUIZ—CELEBRITY SAYINGS

Questions

1. Jackie Vernon said: "My grandfather was an old Indian fighter." What did he say about his grandmother?

2. What happened when Jackie Vernon said to a crowd, "Let he who is without sin cast the first stone"?

3. What comedian said this about Johnny Carson: "His first wife was Joan. His second wife was Joanne. His third wife was Joanna. Here's a guy who didn't get new towels"?

4. What comedian said this about Johnny Carson: "Johnny started out as a magician. Then he made three wives disappear"?

5. Who said this: "I really don't deserve this award, but then I have arthritis and I don't deserve that either"?

6. What Kentucky activist and Christian writer said: "It is probably lucky for man that he was created last. He would have got too excited and upset over all the change"?

7. Which President said: "Fellow citizens, we cannot escape history. ...No personal significance or insignificance can spare one or another of us. The fiery trial through which we pass will light us down in honor or dishonor, to the latest generation. We shall nobly save or meanly lose the last best hope of earth"?

8. What was a Jimmy Stewart's New Years' resolution?

9. Jim Gaffigan is not a big kale fan. He says if it turns out that kale is a cure for cancer, he would say what to the doctor?

10. Who was the colorful, pompous sports journalist who was always "telling it like it is?"

Answers

1. "My grandmother was an old Indian."
2. Someone hit him with a rock.
3. Bob Newhart
4. Johnathan Winter.
5. Jack Benny
6. Wendell Berry
7. Abraham Lincoln
8. To talk faster.
9. "I'll take the chemo."
10. Howard Cosell.

JIM FINKS WITH SISTERS AT TRAINING CAMP

You Shall Not Criticize the Officials.

Introduction

"You shall not criticize the officials" is a tough football commandment. People can get pretty emotional playing, coaching, and watching a game. George Halas would sometimes criticize an official. One time he said to a referee during a game, *"No man is completely worthless; you can always serve as a horrible example."*

If you watch sports you know that the problem with criticizing an official is that it can get out of hand. Just like the players on the field, if the refs come under heavy criticism their performance is likely to get worse, not better. They are human after all.

I could get angry during a game as well and I found the best thing for me to do is to have a pad of paper and just take notes. I did this with my children's games and I will do it again when my grandchildren start playing.

The meaning of this commandment is to **respect authority**. If we lose respect for authority, things fall apart.

Lessons from Odd Places

One of my favorite books is John Powers, *Last Catholic in America*. My wife Gretchen, our children, and I had dinner with Powers at his home in Lake Geneva a few years before he died. Powers liked to say his books were about the Catholic way of life and he was not casting either a positive or negative light on it. Regardless, his stories are funny and there are positive messages in his books. *Last Catholic in America* is a fictional memoir, so parts of it are based on fact.

In *Last Catholic in America*, Powers's pastor is Father O'Brien. He describes Father O'Brien as an intimidating authoritarian figure who moves things along as he sees fit. At one time in the early days of the parish, Father O'Brien had sold chickens door to door to keep the parish afloat. Decades later, parish life and finances had improved. Father O'Brien announces plans to build a new church on vacant church property. Some newer members of the parish get concerned because the building site abuts a decrepit two-flat owned by a local "bag-lady," Garbage Lady Annie. These parishioners say they are going to take action to see that the flat will be torn down. Father O'Brien disagrees. He says that Garbage Lady Annie's home will not be torn down and he dismisses the idea.

The newcomers "criticize the official" (Father O'Brien) and take action to begin the process of condemnation. But the Board of Health and the Building Commission filings are rejected. A petition gets lost at City Hall. The church is built along side of Garbage Lady Annie's home.

A few months later, Father O'Brien dies—an old tradition according to Powers that has to do with priests who build new churches. Years later, Garbage Lady Annie succumbs to old age. Neighbors enter her home. They find evidence that she was providing the chickens that Father O'Brien had sold in the early days of the church. Garbage Lady Annie was much more than a "bag lady."

JIM FINKS

On September 12, 1974, Jim Finks joined the Chicago Bears as the executive vice president, general manager, and chief operating officer. Here is how he built the Bears' 1985 Championship team.

In 1975, he drafted Walter Payton and Mike Hartenstine. In 1976, he signed Gary Fencik as a free agent. In 1979, he drafted Dan Hampton. In 1980, he drafted Otis Wilson and Matt Suhey. In 1981, he drafted Keith Van Horne and Mike Singletary and signed Leslie Frazier, Jay Hilgenberg, Steve McMichael, and Emery Moorehead as free agents. In 1982, he drafted Jim McMahon, Tim Wrightman, Dennis Gentry, Kurt Becker, and Henry Waechter. In 1983, he drafted Jim Covert, Willie Gault, Mike Richardson, Dave Duerson, Tom Thayer, Richard Dent, and Mark Bortz, and he signed Dennis McKinnon as a free agent.

In 1995, my father, Ed McCaskey, presented Jim Finks for induction into the Pro Football Hall of Fame. My father said, Jim was tough but fair and honest, and he believed that building an organization was the key to success on the football field.

"Each year, the Chicago Bears invite their alumni to a dinner and a game in Chicago. Those who can't come sometimes write letters telling of their most memorable experiences as a Bear. Our fearless safety of yesteryear, Doug Plank, wrote of his most memorable experience. It wasn't something that happened on the playing field, but in Jim Finks's office. I would like to read Doug's letter for you.

"Doug wrote, 'I had just completed my third year as a starting safety. Since I was drafted in the 12th round, my salary qualified me for low-income housing. I was attempting to double my salary. After I submitted my initial offer to Jim Finks, he immediately countered with a 50 percent reduction in my increase. Intimidated by his position and his negotiating ability, I explained that I would have to discuss the offer with my wife before making a decision.

'"After my response, the room became quiet, and he stared into my eyes for what seemed an eternity. He eventually responded by saying, 'Doug, go home and talk to your wife, and I will go home and talk to my wife. I want to make certain that I did not offer too much.'"

BEARS' LICENSE PLATES

Ninety-one Chicago Bears have played high school football in the state of Illinois. That includes seven Pro Football Hall of Famers: Dick Butkus at Chicago Vocational, George Connor at De La Salle, Paddy Driscoll at Evanston, Red Grange at Wheaton, George Halas at Crane Tech, George Musso at Collinsville, and George Trafton at Oak Park.

Football team for Illinois,
Play Maker, Stacker of Wins,
Where license plates showcase the Chicago Bears
Championship, Sportsmanship,
State of the Shoulder Pads;
The rush is on. So don't be late. Illinois, Illinois.

You can get a Bears' license plate. Illinois. Illinois.
Jesse White is very great.
He's Secretary of State, Chicago Bears' license plate.
Illinois. Illinois.

SWEETNESS AT THE TOP

Walter Payton is right at the top of many sports analysts' lists of the best players in NFL history. In 13 seasons, Payton had 3,838 rushes for 16,726 yards and 110 rushing touchdowns. Payton had 492 receptions for 4,538 yards and 15 touchdowns. For his 13 years of work, he had a 4.4 yard per carry average. He led the league in rushing from 1976 to 1980. He only missed one game in his entire career. In the Bears Super Bowl year 1985, his 11th season, he only gained 1,551 yards and scored 9 rushing touchdowns!

Sadly, Walter Payton died young at age 45 on November 1, 1999. He was a "Monster of the Midway," "Sweetness" 'till the end. It's been said, *"We know what people have been and in a sense what they have done, only when we know how they have died."*[76]

POEM FOR THE AUTHOR BY NANCY LAUZON

As you sat on your Grandpa's knee,
You thought you knew your destiny.
In the playbook of life, you were the man.
You worked really hard to fulfill your plan.
In football and track you became a star.
Armed with success, you knew you'd go far.

But God in His Majestic Will,
Had other shoes for you to fill.
In His Divine Sight, He saw in your seeing,
Some problems that led to a new way of being.
Knowing in life, how you trip and fall,
You got back up and answered His Call.
With God the Divine Coach in the lead,
You found other ways for you to succeed.
With all different hats, you work for the Bears,
And always show others how much God cares.
Your playbook may not be what you had planned,
But it is written by the Master's Hand.
When you speak for Him, there's never a loss.
For He loves us all, while His Son paid the cost!

FATHER AUGUSTUS TOLTON

FATHER TOLTON

On April 1, 1854, Augustus Tolton was born in Brush Creek, Rails County, Missouri. His parents were slaves. He was baptized at Saint Peter's Catholic Church in Brush Creek.

The Toltons fled to Illinois because it was a free state. They worked in a cigar factory in Quincy. Thanks to Father McGirr, during the winter months, when the tobacco factory was closed, Augustus attended Saint Peter's School. Then some priests taught him directly.

Augustus graduated from Saint Francis Solanus College, which is now Quincy University. Then he attended the Pontifical Urbaniana University in Rome where he studied Greek and Latin and became fluent in Italian.

On April 24, 1886, Holy Saturday, he was ordained a priest. The following day he celebrated his first Mass at Saint Peter's Basilica in Rome on Easter day. He was directed to return to the United States and serve the black community. Before arriving in the States, he said Mass at several of the great cathedrals and shrines of Europe. His first Mass on American soil was at St. Benedict the Moor parish church located at Bleeker and Downing Streets in New York City. He organized Saint Joseph Catholic Church and School in Quincy.[77]

After Father Tolton had been assigned to Chicago, he was the pastor of Saint Monica's Catholic Church at 36th and Dearborn Streets on the South Side of Chicago. His sermons were eloquent; his singing was beautiful; and he played the accordion. His example of faithfulness and forgiveness inspired many other black men to enter seminaries.

On July 9, 1897, Father Tolton died in Chicago. As he had requested, he was buried at Saint Peter's Cemetery in Quincy.

On March 2, 2010, Francis Cardinal George began the quest to have Father Tolton declared a saint. On February 24, 2011, Cardinal George assigned Bishop Joseph Perry to do the research. Bishop Perry was obedient. On December 10, 2016, Father Tolton's remains were exhumed; it was part of the canonization process. An icon of Fr. Tolton was commissioned by Bishop Perry and created by Chicago iconographer, Joseph Malham of Trinity Icons.[78]

Since exhumation is part of canonization, I am not interested in cremation.

On November 5, 2017, a play about his life, "Tolton: From Slave to Priest," was at the DuSable Museum Institute Theater on the South Side of Chicago. Bishop Perry did the welcome. Marist High School Senior Peyton Ashford said the opening prayer. Andrae Goodnight played Father Tolton. Elissa Sanders played his mother, Martha Jane Tolton. Michael Lee played Father McGirr. Leonardo Defilippis of Saint Luke Productions was the director. It was magnificent.

LETTER FROM DAN ROONEY

Dan Rooney died on Seamus Heaney's birthday, April 13, 2017. Seamus Heaney died on August 30, 2013, on the feast day of Saint Rumon, an Irish Missionary.

In the summer of 1995, Seamus Heaney was on a working vacation in Greece. When he called home to see if there was anything new, his son said, "*Yes, you won the Nobel Prize for Literature.*"

He grew up in County Derry in Northern Ireland. He and his brothers played football in a field at the back of their home. In his poem "Markings," he wrote that they put down "four jackets for four goalposts." They played until "the light died."

> And the actual kicked ball came to them
> Like a dream heaviness, and their own hard
> Breathing in the dark and skids on grass
> Sounded like effort in another world…

After I had sent the poem to Dan Rooney, he wrote this letter to me.

11 January 2000

Dear Patrick:

Seamus Heaney is an excellent person in addition to being Poet Laureate in Britain and Ireland.

His markings piece, especially about what we will call a game of touch, is quite memorable. It takes us back to our youth. I have used this often in talks.

I do appreciate you thinking of me and sending it.

We are taking our family back to Ireland this summer. It will be a grand time. Give our best to Big Ed and Virginia.

Good luck with your team!

All the Best,

Dan Rooney

Resolution for Sharon Lehner

STATE OF ILLINOIS

COUNTY OF LAKE

RESOLUTION

WHEREAS, Sharon Lehner began working for the Chicago Bears on January 29, 1998, and

WHEREAS, Sharon Lehner never sued the Chicago Bears, and

WHEREAS, Sharon Lehner cared very much about the Chicago Bears, and

WHEREAS, Sharon Lehner helped the Chicago Bears to win every possible game because she felt that excuses were lame, and

WHEREAS, Sharon Lehner was not a complainer, and

WHEREAS, we did not ask why she married that guy, and

WHEREAS, no other one could ever take the place of Sharon Lehner, and

WHEREAS, Sharon Lehner, Jessica Noonan, and Kate Rackow are a cross between The Trinity and the three stooges, and

WHEREAS, we are glad that you worked here and we thank you for your cheer.

NOW THEREFORE BE IT RESOLVED that the Chicago

Bears adopt this Resolution to honor and hold in high esteem
Sharon Lehner.

Adopted the first day of June, 2017.

RESOLUTION FOR DAVE HALE

STATE OF ILLINOIS

COUNTY OF LAKE

RESOLUTION

WHEREAS, David Robert Hale was born June 21, 1947, in
McCook, Nebraska, and

WHEREAS, Dave matriculated at Ottawa University, and

WHEREAS, Dave lettered eight times total in three sports—
football-3, basketball-2, and track-3, and

WHEREAS, Dave was the NAIA champion in the discus,
and

WHEREAS, Dave graduated with a BA in Chemistry, and

WHEREAS, Dave was a 12th round draft choice of the
Chicago Bears in 1969, and

WHEREAS, Dave played for the Bears from 1969 through
1973, and

WHEREAS, Dave and his wife, Nori, have five children and
13 grandchildren, and

WHEREAS, Dave admits that Jesus died for his sins, and

WHEREAS, Dave was the Chicago Director of the
Fellowship of Christian Athletes, and

WHEREAS, Dave is a successful businessman.

NOW THEREFORE BE IT RESOLVED that the Chicago Bears adopt this Resolution to honor and hold in high esteem Dave Hale.

Adopted the 21st day of June, 2017.

RESOLUTION FOR FATHER JAMNICKY

STATE OF ILLINOIS

COUNTY OF LAKE

RESOLUTION

WHEREAS, John Jamnicky walked a mile to attend Saint Francis de Sales Grade School on the Southeast Side, and

WHEREAS, John Jamnicky was in wrestling and basketball at Quigley North and South Seminaries, and

WHEREAS, John Jamnicky had quite a few jobs at Republic and Wisconsin Steel, before and during Niles Seminary, and

WHEREAS, John Jamnicky was given a year away from Mundelein for a course in clinical pastoral education, and

WHEREAS, John Jamnicky has a bachelor's in philosophy and a masters in divinity from University of Saint Mary of the Lake, and

WHEREAS, John Jamnicky was ordained a priest in 1972, and

WHEREAS, Father Jamnicky was assigned to Saint Martin's Parish on Chicago's South Side, and

WHEREAS, Father Jamnicky was Chaplain of O'Hare Airport Chapel, and

WHEREAS, Father Jamnicky was Chaplain to the Illinois National Guard and U.S. Air Force with the rank of Captain, and

WHEREAS, Father Jamnicky was National Coordinator for Mobility Associates in Washington, D.C., and

WHEREAS, Father Jamnicky spent a six-month sabbatical ministering in Alaska, and

WHEREAS, Father Jamnicky was the pastor of Saint Raphael the Archangel in Antioch, and

WHEREAS, Father Jamnicky was very helpful to WSFI-88.5 FM Catholic Radio.

NOW THEREFORE BE IT RESOLVED that the Chicago Bears adopt this Resolution to honor and hold in high esteem Father Jamnicky.

Adopted the 24th day of June, 2017.

SAINT VINCENT DE PAUL

Saint Vincent de Paul was born on April 24, 1581, in the southwest corner of France in a town now appropriately called Saint-Vincent-de-Paul. His birthplace is about 70 miles from Saint Jean Pied de Port the traditional starting place for the French Way of Saint James—the long trek that a quarter million pilgrims take to the Cathedral at Compostela.[79] Vincent's efforts to help the poor and his ability to establish a charitable mindset with the rich was something that would have made the *Guinness Book of World Records*.

Vincent was bright, humble, and born of peasant stock. At the same time, he had an irritable personality that he was able to tame with help from above. His life was Forest Gump-like and included many extraordinary experiences. He was compassionate, reform-minded, and fought heresy.

Vincent tutored children of wealthy parents, which allowed him to continue his studies and work towards becoming a priest. School apparently was not cheap in those days either. After his ordination in 1600, he continued his studies.

On his way back from Marseilles traveling by sea in 1605, Turkish pirates captured him and sold him as a slave in Africa. Vincent was bought and sold several times over a few years, but he eventually escaped.[80]

Vincent's studies were extensive and included time in Rome. He went to Paris, where he remained permanently. He acted as a spiritual adviser and worked with the wealthy including royalty to handle alms. Vincent encouraged people from high places to consider the suffering and needs of the poor.

One of the Saint's passions was providing spiritual counsel and physical care to prisoners-for-life who were housed in dungeons and served as galley slaves. Eventually, Vincent became a leader and founder of the Congregation of the Mission, or the Vincentians—priests, with vows of poverty, chastity, obedience, and stability. He drew up rules and constitutions that were approved by Pope Urban VIII in 1632.

Later, Vincent established associations of charitable lay people to help the spiritual and physical relief of the poor and sick of each parish. From these, along with Saint Louise de Marillac, came the Daughters of Charity.[81] He organized wealthy women of Paris to collect funds for his missionary projects, found hospitals, and gather money to help the other victims in society. He reenergized a lax clergy, developed improved training, and established seminaries. He was a force!

Pope Leo XIII made him the patron of all charitable societies. Outstanding among these, of course, is the Society of Saint Vincent de Paul, founded in 1833 by Blessed Frédéric Ozanam. The Society has about 800,000 members world-wide in 150 countries. In the United States, there are about 100,000 members in 4,400 communities.[82]

Saint Vincent died September 27, 1660, in Paris. Buried in the church of Saint Lazare, Paris, he was canonized by Clement XII in 1737. His feast day is September 27.

Quiz—Bears Not for Faint-Hearted

Questions

1. Who was the Bears 1st round draft pick in 1999 who had a remarkable college career at quarterback at UCLA and visited John Wooden for five-hours at his home?
2. Which '85 Bear defensive tackle is least likely to write for Hallmark?
3. This Bears head coach can be seen on the last episode of the popular TV Show, "Cheers."
4. Saint Joseph's College, Lake Forest College, and Conway Business Park in Lake Forest all have a facility called what?

5.   When was the George Halas Trophy first presented to the NFC champions?

6.   On what street is the Pro Football Hall of Fame located?

7.   Is George Halas's image on postage stamps?

8.   When did George Halas's home (as the Bears began in Chicago) receive a marker of distinction?

9.   Are there more than 25 Bears or less than 25 Bears inducted into the Pro Football Hall of Fame?

10. Which four Bear quarterbacks have played in the Pro Bowl?

Answers

1.   The Bears 1st round draft pick in 1999 was Cade McNown.

2.   Steve McMichael

3.   Mike Ditka

4.   All three have a Halas Hall. Saint Joseph's College Halas Hall was established in 1958. Halas Hall at Lake Forest College opened in August 1979. Halas Hall at Conway Business Park in Lake Forest, which serves as the current home to the Bears was opened on Monday, March 3, 1997.

5.   January 1985

6.   George Halas Drive was running in June 1985.

7.   George Halas was placed on stamps in August 17, 1997.

8.   George Halas's home when he started the Bears in Chicago received a marker of distinction on September 23, 1997.

9. Twenty-eight Bears have been inducted into the Pro Football Hall of Fame (most recent is Brian Urlacher).
10. The four Bear quarterbacks who have played in the Pro Bowl are Johnny Lujack, Ed Brown, Bill Wade, and Jim McMahon.

You Shall Not Covet Other Teams' Coaches or Players.

Introduction

It's OK to seek players and coaches as their contracts end or as they move up from college to the pros. In early NFL history, many teams wanted college sensation Red Grange. The league was just a few years along and George Halas made a deal with Grange and his agent C. C. Pyle that might remind people today of many modern agreements. Grange got a piece of the gate receipts!

In 1938, Art Rooney, owner of the Steelers, went after a Rhodes Scholar by the name of Byron "Whizzer" White who was another magnificent player. White postponed his studies for a year and was paid handsomely for his services, $15,800. Later he would go on to serve on the Supreme Court. Seeking the best is part of competition, an important part.

But in life, if we are not well grounded, we can want what others have, but never find our true calling. We can see others and "want to be them." In *Sports and Faith: Stories of the Devoted and the Devout*, I wrote briefly about the Shaker Hymn, "Simple Gifts," and about how George Halas sought out **his** place and was not satisfied until he found it. We all need to find **our** place—to do the work we are called to do. We need to keep "turning and turning" until we find ourselves "in the place just right." Halas worked in many capacities before he found professional football and then he held on for decades before it paid off. The meaning of this commandment is **"find your own calling."**

Long's Worthwhile Struggle

At the 2014 Pro Bowl in Hawaii, my wife, Gretchen, and I had dinner with a group of Bears' Pro Bowlers including Kyle Long. I am glad the Bears have Kyle Long. His dad, Howie Long, is a Hall of Famer.

Howie Long's early life in the Charlestown section of Boston was difficult—his neighborhood was made up mostly of proud struggling Irish who worked hard to make a living.[83] During High School, he lived with his Aunt Aida and Uncle Billy in Milford, Massachusetts. Long attended Villanova University on scholarship, where he was a 4-year letterman in football. He married his college sweetheart, Diane Addonizio, who was tops in her class at Villanova. She is an attorney.

The 6-foot-5, 268-pound defensive end was a second round draft pick of the Oakland Raiders in 1981. Howie contributed mightily to the 1983 Raiders' success and its 38–9 Super Bowl XV win over the Washington Redskins. Howie was inducted into the Pro Football Hall of Fame as a member of the class of 2000.

For Howie, football provided a means for self-esteem, discipline, and respect. He believes that football can help provide structure in a young man's life, and experiences with a team are also helpful. All three of Long's sons have played football.[84] Long was brought up as a Catholic and his grandmother was a great influence on him. Long was long on desire and work ethic. He thanks others for his success:

"God gave me good people around me, and He gave me size. It's kind of a miracle, really."[85]

Long's sons, Chris, Kyle, and Howie Jr. have followed their dad into the NFL. Chris is a 6-foot-4, 275 pound defensive end who has won Super Bowls with the New England Patriots and the Philadelphia Eagles. Youngest son Howie Jr. has worked in player personnel for the Raiders.

Kyle is a 6-foot-6, 315 pound offensive lineman for the Chicago Bears. Kyle Long was selected by the Bears with the 20th pick in the first round of the 2013 draft out of Oregon. Kyle was a Pro-Bowl guard for his first three seasons, but has been plagued by injuries in the last two.

Kyle Long was honored as the Bears' recipient of the Ed Block Courage Award at a luncheon at Maryville Academy in Des Plaines in 2018. The Ed Block Courage Award is presented to one player on each NFL team who exemplifies a commitment to sportsmanship and courage. Teammates vote to determine the recipient.

Ed Block was a long-time head trainer with the Baltimore Colts—a pioneer in his field. The Ed Block Courage Award Foundation assists agencies that provide for the care and treatment of abused children. The luncheon event itself raises funds for the Ed McCaskey Scholarship which pays for high school, college, and vocational scholarships for the children of Maryville. The prestigious awards are presented to one player on all 32 NFL teams.

Despite suffering injuries, Long has demonstrated an intense competitive spirit and courage as a member of the Bears. Speaking to reporters after receiving the reward, Kyle said:

"It's a tremendous honor to be here today. I think the more that we can do for others, the better off we'll be for ourselves.

Any impact we can have on another person's life and an opportunity to go to bat for somebody who can't go to bat for themselves is something that I stand up for. I'm very happy to be here today, humbled to be voted here by my teammates and my peers. I'm just a microcosm of the locker room. We have many, many guys who could be here today in my shoes."

TOM O'HARA AT SAINT IGNATIUS

Tom O'Hara

Runners are often spiritual people. They accept suffering. And before there were gyms and recreation centers around every corner, runners ached through the seasons in places like Chicago where the weather can be cruelly cold in winter or hellishly hot in summer.

Tom O'Hara was one of those runners who could not stay off the Chicago streets, alleys, parks, and paths. They led from his family's modest Bucktown apartment to world records.

Athletes like O'Hara cannot live without such suffering and accomplishment. Nora O'Hara, Tom's mother said, *"running is like Lent to Tom."*[86]

A running career can be short, but Tom O'Hara continued running into his 70s. It was his calling. In his college days, it was daily runs and a quick stop at the Loyola Food Shop for a ham sandwich (cheese on Fridays). Later, running was an after-hours passion when he went to work selling insurance.

Tom O'Hara ran cross country and track for Saint Ignatius College Prep and Loyola University in Chicago. For Saint Ignatius, he ran and won the quarter mile, the half mile, the mile, and the mile relay all in the same meets.

For Loyola, he was a national champion in cross country and the 1500 meter run. Tom O'Hara was the first native of the state of Illinois to break the four-minute mile barrier when he ran 3:59.4 in 1963 for Loyola University. He broke the indoor record for the world's fastest mile, when he ran 3:56.6 on February 13, 1964. He beat that record on March 6 of the same year with a time of 3:56.4, a world record that stood for 10 years.

Described in the press as "a pale redhead" and in *Life* (Feb. 21, 1964) as "someone who looks like he might come unglued as he runs," O'Hara astounded reporters for how he blew away the field at times in both high school and college. He qualified for the 1964 Olympic team, but was sick and did not medal. O'Hara was inducted into the Sports Faith International Hall of Fame

Journalist Robert Creamer wrote, *"The pale, skinny, slump-shouldered kid from Chicago—standing around in a hotel lobby before a meet...looks more like a bellhop than an athlete."*[87] During his races, *"he hitched up his pants, a characteristic gesture he makes several times a race, to the delight of the fans, and went to work."*

When my grandfather, George Halas, was coaching the Chicago Bears, the players had to start training camp with the Halas Mile. That's how I got interested in running and Tom O'Hara. I encountered O'Hara on the Lake Michigan Chicago Lakefront.

When the Bears' offices were at 55 East Jackson in Chicago, I ran home along the Lake to 2000 North.

One evening, another runner, who had seen me running before, caught up to me to ask why I was doing so much running. I recognized him as O'Hara and so I said, *"I've always admired Tom O'Hara."*

SAINT ANTHONY

SAINT ANTHONY, FINDER OF LOST ARTICLES

Saint Anthony of Padua was a Franciscan. At a Dominican ordination, the Franciscans thought that a Dominican would give the homily. The Dominicans thought that a Franciscan would preach. The head of the hermitage asked Saint Anthony to say whatever the Holy Spirit would put in his mouth.[88] Listeners were amazed at Anthony's homily although created on the spot. After Saint Francis had heard about Saint Anthony's homily, he asked Saint Anthony to teach theology.

Saint Anthony had a book of psalms with his notes and comments for teaching. The book was valuable because the printing press had not been invented yet. Someone stole the book; Saint Anthony prayed that it would be found or returned. The thief returned the book. That's why we pray to Saint Anthony when things are lost. In 1231, Saint Anthony died on June 13, which is his feast day.

RED GRANGE, COVETED RUNNING BACK

On June 13, Saint Anthony's feast day, Red Grange was born in 1903. While astounding football fans at the University of Illinois, Grange achieved notoriety and many professional football teams wanted him. Grange scored 6 touchdowns in a game against Michigan. He became a cultural icon. His photo was on the cover of Time Magazine on October 5, 1925.

University of Illinois alum, George Halas came, saw, and signed him on Sunday, November 22, 1925. That same day, the Bears played the Green Bay Packers at Wrigley Field. The Bears won, 21–0. The NFL needed a spark and Grange was it. From November 26, 1925, through January 31, 1926, the Bears went on a coast-to-coast tour and played 19 games. This gave pro football national recognition and helped improve the financial condition of the teams.

After the Red Grange Tour, Grange's agent, C. C. Pyle wanted a third interest in the Bears going into the following season. After my grandfather had turned him down, Pyle started his own league, the first American Football League, and he took Grange with him.

After the AFL had folded, Pyle's team joined the NFL. On Sunday, October 16, 1927, the Bears played the New York Yankees at Wrigley Field. Grange played for the Yankees and he got hurt. The Bears won, 12–0.

Grange was out of football in 1928. He came back to the Bears in 1929. He couldn't cut like he used to, but he was a good defensive back.

He played on the Bears' 1932 and 1933 NFL Championship Teams. An All-Pro three times, he made the NFL 1920s All-Decade Team. Grange was a Bears' assistant coach for the 1933 and 1940 NFL Championship Teams. He was a Bears' broadcaster. He is a Pro Football Hall of Famer. His Bears' number, 77, is retired.

RESPECTFUL COMIC RELIEF

My grandfather was in the Navy during World War I and World War II. We won both wars.

My father had heard that Hitler's ultimate plan was the capture of Ireland. So, my father defeated Hitler with a sling and five smooth stones.

It was my father's idea for players to room together based on position. Brian Piccolo, a white player, and Gale Sayers, a black player, were the first integrated roommates. When Brian Piccolo saw a white player between two black players, he would call them a human Oreo.

For my last two semesters at Indiana University, I lived in a sorority with 70 ladies as their houseboy. I gave that up to work for the Bears. Craig Clemons, a black player, taught me the eight-step handshake.

The last 5 years of Grandpa's life, his grandchildren took him out to dinner on his birthday. On Wednesday, February 2, 1983, his 88th birthday, we should have known that something was amiss because he told us that he did not swear anymore. He also said, *"May the Good Lord grant all of you as long and as wonderful a life as I have had."*

There is nothing dumber than prejudice. We are here to live the Gospel.

When I was studying for the SATs, I learned the word tautology: t-a-u-t-o-l-o-g-y. It means unnecessary repetition.

After a Bears' loss, Brandon Marshall used the word **unacceptable** 17 times. Then I taught him the word tautology.

The Garden of Eden was closed a long time ago. If we wait until the United States is perfect before we honor it, we'll never be able to do it.

CATHOLIC NEW WORLD ALL AREA TEAM

On December 24, 1966, my sister, Mary, and I stayed with my grandfather, George Halas, at the Edgewater Beach Apartments in Chicago. It was the first Christmas Eve after our grandmother had died. I read in the *Chicago American* that I had made the *Catholic New World* All Area team. Here is the complete lineup with their stats and head coach listed:

E *Frank Butler, Leo, 6-foot-4, 195 pounds, Bob Hanlon*
E *Steve Flanagan, Fenwick, 6-foot-2, 190 pounds, Len Tyrell*
E *Tom Neiman, Loyola, 6-foot-1, 190 pounds, Bob Naughton*
T *Steve Lawson, Mount Carmel, 6-foot-2, 240 pounds, Frank Maloney*
T *Ron Curl, De La Salle, 6-foot-2, 225, pounds, Pat Cronin*
G *Pete Newell, Notre Dame, 6-foot-4, 215 pounds, Fran Willett*
G *Bill Drury, Saint Patrick, 6-foot-1, 210 pounds, Fred Dempsey*
C *Paul Panczuk, Saint Francis de Sales, 6-foot-1, 205 pounds,*
   Bill Styczynski
QB *Pat McCaskey, Notre Dame, 6-foot-1, 190 pounds, Fran Willett*
B *Randy Marks, Loyola, 5-foot-11, 201 pounds, Bob Naughton*
B *Tom Shinnick, De La Salle, 6-foot, 180 pounds, Pat Cronin*
B *Dan Kelly, Little Flower, 6-foot, 170 pounds, Jack Lord*

From *Catholic New World*, we know that, the line averaged out better than 219 pounds per man from tackle to tackle. The five front guys had gone both ways—offensively and defensively—all season.

The three backs totaled more than 40 touchdowns that season. The quarterback was the principal engineer of an offense that rolled up 290 points in seven conference games.

Three ends—Butler of Leo, Flanagan of Fenwick, and Neiman of Loyola were in a class by themselves. Neiman proved to be a real defensive sparkplug for the Ramblers en route to their second straight all-city crown. His aggressiveness didn't end on defense either.

Butler and Flanagan also went both ways, the former proving himself quite an adroit pass-catcher. Their play was one of the big pushes that carried both Leo and Fenwick into the Catholic League semifinals.

Every one of the four interior linemen on the squad—Drury of Saint Patrick, Newell of Notre Dame, Curl of De La Salle, and Lawson of Mount Carmel—were hard-hitting blockers on offense and they totaled almost 500 tackles among them during the season. That breaks down to about a 12 tackles per game average.[89]

Center Panczuk played 25 games over three seasons at Saint Frances de Sales, recording 1,162 minutes of playing time, out of a possible 1,200. Over the three seasons, he caused no less than 25 fumbles while leading the team in tackles twice.

The three running backs on the squad scored more than 40 touchdowns, a total which broke down to 17 for Marks of Loyola, 15 for Kelly of Little Flower, and 14 for Shinnick of De La Salle.

Marks took both scoring and rushing honors in the Catholic League, as did Shinnick in the Chicagoland Prep League. Kelly totaled more than 1,200 yards with the best team in Little Flower's short football history.

I was defensive signal caller, right outside linebacker, blocking back on the punts, and quarterback of the Notre Dame team that was 9–0 and outscored opponents 341–80.

CARDINAL GEORGE

What a difference that God makes
He was almighty powers
Made the sun and the flowers
He also provides rain

My yesterday was blue, God
Today I'm part of you, God
My lonely nights are through, God
Since we have been entwined

What a difference that God makes
There's a rainbow before me
Even when skies are stormy
We have the Cardinal's book, that well-written book

It's heaven when you find mercy on your menu
What a difference that God makes
And the difference is grace

In Cardinal George's book, *A Godly Humanism: Clarifying the Hope That Lies Within*, he pointed out that Saint Pope John Paul II continued to write poetry after he had been named Pope.

I not only read Cardinal George's books, I bought them. We were grateful to Cardinal George for his support of Sports Faith International and WSFI 88.5 FM Catholic Radio. Cardinal George was an excellent man of God.

THE AFFECTIONATE DOUBLE CART WHEELERS

If male and female were unicellular, each organism would have four arms, four legs, and two heads. They would proceed down the street by means of double cart wheels. Hands closest to the ground would be used for balance, while the opposite hands would be used for picking flowers and snapping their fingers.

Marital strife would be almost completely non-existent. Bickering would be on the level of only one on a ten-point scale. Then these organisms would be divided into half male and half female.

As a result, men and women would be compelled to look for their other halves. The search would be long and exhausting because they had to travel on their own and could not use double cart wheels.

Mistakes in the selecting process would be made, for even in the realm of science there is room for human error. A bad selection is where bickering increases as the years go by instead of lessens.

Happily married couples would become the most significant minority group. In an attempt to recapture the utter euphoria of double cart wheels, teachers would teach that double cart wheels were good and wholesome with your other half.

People would begin not only to show their children in home movies, but also how they were conceived.

Double cart wheels would be sought for their own sake with anyone and not as a physical expression for your other half. Test tubes would be used to produce children in order to avoid the messiness of getting involved emotionally and then committing yourself to another person.

Finally, a group of radicals would discover that attempts at double cart wheels with someone other than their half only produced clumsiness.

Then they would agree to try something new and different. They would only have double cart wheels with their other halves. (They would have them in the privacy of their own homes.)

In each unique relationship two beings would become one and yet remain two. Although their marriages and their families would have ups and downs, they would feel that love was a worthwhile struggle.

TEAMS WANTED GUY CHAMBERLIN

Guy Chamberlin won his NFL Championships in the 1920s. He was a brainy player and coach for championship teams— teams that no longer exist: The Canton Bulldogs, the Cleveland Bulldogs, and the Frankford Yellow Jackets. His NFL reputation has grown dim over the years because he has no NFL base like coaches whose teams have carried on to this day. He is one of the ten coaches who have won three or more NFL Championships, but he is an NFL orphan.

Chamberlin was also a great college player.[90] The University of Nebraska recognizes great players with the Chamberlin Award. The award is presented to the senior player who has shown by his play and contributions to the team that he has the qualities and dedication of Guy Chamberlin to the Cornhusker tradition.

Recent efforts to rekindle his reputation as one of the NFL's greatest coaches have been building. Folks back home in Gage County Nebraska have worked to see Chamberlin recognized and remembered.

Chamberlin was an exceptional player and a winner. Chamberlin was part of 5 championship teams in the NFL. As a player-coach he won 4 championships and won one as a player under Coach George Halas of the Chicago Staleys (soon to be Bears) in 1921. His wins all came in a brief 8-year career. Chamberlin played end on defense and offense in the pros.

Passing was not prevalent as it is today, but Chamberlin kept things exciting with his end-around runs that showcased his speed and power. And in a flash, defensive end Chamberlin was in the opposing backfield destroying plays before they began. Excellent on special teams as well, he frequently foiled the opposing team's punt returns with a strong sprint down the field and a swift tackle.

George Halas also played end at the time Chamberlin played. He knew the position well. According to Halas:

He [Chamberlin] *had all the attributes of a great football player and as you can imagine in those early days players were far more rugged than they are today...professional football was very fortunate in having a man of his caliber as one of its pioneers.*

Unlike some other players and coaches like George Halas and Curly Lambeau, Chamberlin thought professional football would not last. But Chamberlin loved the game of football. He was the consummate country boy who grew up to be sturdy, speedy, and exceptionally competitive.

Chamberlin attended Nebraska Wesleyan and then the University of Nebraska. Through college and pros, *"there was never a guy who liked to play football as well as he did."*[91] Chamberlin was enshrined in the Pro Football Hall of Fame and the College Hall of Fame. He accepted his honors with great humility.

As a college student, Chamberlin taught Sunday school at the First Methodist Church. He was a college track star. He played baseball as well. After the pros, he eventually returned to work around his family farm.

SAINT COLUMBA

St Columba was born about 521 AD in County Donegal, Ireland. He is one of the great monks of Ireland, but he also came to be loved in Scotland. His feast day is June 9.

Saint Columba was sent away to school where he learned among other things, about his culture, songs, and poetry. When he became a man he was sent to a famous monastic school called Clonard that was run by Saint Finnian. At Finnian's school there were thousands of students and some who would become legends in the church. Columba would go on to become one of the Twelve Apostles of Erin. These 6th century Irish Apostles are:

St. Ciaran of Saighir

St. Ciaran of Clonmacnois

St. Brendan of Birr

St. Brendan of Clonfert (the Navigator)

St. Columba of Terryglass

St. Columba of Iona

St. Mobhi of Glasnevin

St. Ruadhan of Lorrha

St. Senan of Scattery Island

St. Ninnidh the Saintly of Loch Erne

St. Lasserian mac Nadfraech

St. Canice of Aghaboe[92]

Columba also went to study under Saint Mobhi as well. He left Saint Mobhi to go back home when he was 25 years old. He had studied well and he had become a priest.

Saint Columba came from royal families on both his mother's and father's side. He was an impressive man and a great speaker. He preached and founded monasteries in Ireland at places like Derry, Durrow, and Kells.

The monks valued books and wanted to preserve learning. Many of the Irish monks were copying manuscripts creating new books as works of art. They were producing what is called illuminated manuscripts. These often included initials, where they would make the first letter of a page or a paragraph larger and decorate it with colored ink and designs. Illuminators might also decorate the borders with artistic designs or embellishments often having to do with the contents. And they would include small miniature images of sacred subjects. These monks would continue to do so at the various monasteries for 300 years—preserving many rare books for history and creating priceless art we can see today.

The Book of Kells, which is the most famous illuminated manuscript, is said to come from one of the monasteries of Saint Columba, the Kells Monastery.

The books the monks copied could come from far away. Columba's old teacher, Finnian, came back from Rome with a copy of a book of Psalms. Such books were guarded like treasure at the time. Columba got to look at the book and made a copy, but he did not have permission to do so. This upset Finnian and he told Columba to give him the copy *that he made*. The dispute went before King Dairmaid who ruled that Columba had no right to copy the book and it should be taken from Columba. The King said, "to every cow his calf and to every book his son book." People look at this as one of the first copyright cases.

Things went from bad to worse. An injured man came to Columba to seek sanctuary. King Dairmaid's men came and took him away and killed him in defiance of the right of sanctuary. So Columba's clan and the King's men faced each other in an armed battle. Columba's Clan prevailed, but 3000 men were killed. A church synod or assembly of authorities met to determine the fate of Columba. The group agreed to censure or express their disapproval to Columba and some wanted to excommunicate him. But another monk, Brendan of Birr spoke up for Columba—telling them that Columba was held in high esteem by God.

Saint Columba decided he would move away from Ireland and seek to convert thousands of people in Scotland. There he would go on to found his celebrated monastery at Iona, an island in the Inner Hebrides off the coast of Scotland. He went on to create many other monasteries in Scotland where he is loved in many.

SPARTAN STADIUM PORTSMOUTH OHIO

QUIZ—BEARS' SERIOUS FANS

Questions

1. What famous Bears' player said the following before his first game as head coach: "All you have to do is want it as much as you know you want it. Do you want it that much?"
2. What five championship games did the Bears lose?
3. Who presented Gale Sayers, George Connor, and George Musso for induction into the Pro Football Hall of Fame?
4. Who presented Bill George, Doug Atkins, and Jim Finks for induction into the Pro Football Hall of Fame?
5. How many Bears have played in the Pro Bowl?
6. What Bears' Coach said the following before the start of the 1946 training camp: "You men have had a lot of discipline during the War. For the next year, all training

rules are off. You All Americans have an equal chance to make the team"?

7. On December 18, 1932, the Bears played the Portsmouth Spartans for the NFL Championship in Chicago. What was so unusual about the game?

8. Who was the College Hall of Fame head coach of the University of Illinois who greatly inspired George Halas?

9. Comedian Joe E. Brown was a Bears fan and Halas said the Bears never lost when Brown sat where?

10. Luke Johnsos and Hunk Anderson co-coached the Bears for a few years. Johnsos recalled "We held tryouts at Cubs Park and signed up everyone who could run around the park twice." Why were the standards so lax?

Answers

1. Mike Ditka
2. 1934, 1937, 1942, 1956, and 2006
3. George Halas
4. Ed McCaskey
5. 86
6. George Halas. The Bears won the championship that season.
7. It was the first indoor NFL football game played and it was played at Chicago Stadium because it had snowed heavily just before the contest.
8. Robert Zuppke.
9. On the Bears bench.
10. They were coaching in WWII while Halas was in the Navy and most players were in the service.

SAINT PATRICK'S CATHEDRAL NEW YORK

GAME TIMES ARE TENTATIVE AND SUBJECT TO FLEXIBLE SCHEDULING.

INTRODUCTION

When you think of professional football, you might have images of huge coaching staffs. You might think of the many players on a team that include everyday players, those on injured reserve, and the practice squad. You might think of the front office and all the people it takes to manage the business affairs of a team. You might also think of the media—those media people inside the organization and those who are the outside media presence—watching everything that goes on with the team. Certainly, there are schedules, to-do-lists, and project managers who look over everything. Yet, those of us involved with a team see a lot of "curve balls." Game times are tentative and subject to flexible scheduling. This is especially true in today's world. The meaning of this commandment is **in order to succeed you need to be flexible and adapt to change**.

GALLOPING GALE SAYERS CARRYING THE MAIL

Gale Sayers was a remarkable player. Exceptionally elusive, he used every inch of his body to twist and turn through defensive lines and past their best players. Sayers could see or sense everyone around him on the field. Once beyond the line of scrimmage, he could accelerate through almost any size hole to daylight. And his moves seemed perfectly choreographed for the budding television audience—reels of highlight films followed him. His career was short—five productive seasons and two cut short with injuries and rehab.

Sayers did everything he could to recover from his 1968 injury. He showed great courage and came back strong. A few years later, in 1970, he was injured again and his career was effectively over. For fans, the Kansas Comet was pure joy to watch. Those who got to see Sayers on the field, will never forget him. Those who played against him would hardly question his Hall of Fame status. Pulitzer Prize sportswriter, Red Smith, called Sayers the most exciting runner of his time.[93]

When my eye doctor, Jonathan Rubenstein, was a boy, he went to the Bears' games with his father. Jonathan's sister complained that she never got to go to a game. The weather happened to be cold and rainy on Sunday, December 12, 1965, so Jonathan said that his sister could go to the game versus the San Francisco 49ers in his place.

Jonathan undoubtedly wished he could have attended the game his sister witnessed. The Bears throttled the 49ers, 61–20, as Sayers scored six touchdowns. Cited as one of the greatest NFL performances, the game kept scorers and reporters busy throughout.

In the first quarter, Rudy Bukich threw an 80-yard touchdown pass to Sayers. Bukich threw a 29-yard touchdown pass to Mike Ditka. Roger Leclerc kicked the extra point. In the second quarter, Sayers had a 21-yard touchdown run. Leclerc kicked the extra point. Sayers had a 7-yard touchdown run. Leclerc kicked the extra point. In the third quarter, Sayers had a 50-yard touchdown run. Leclerc kicked the extra point. Sayers had a 1-yard touchdown run. In the fourth quarter, Bukich threw an 8-yard touchdown pass to Jimmy Jones. Leclerc kicked the extra point. Sayers had an 85-yard punt return for a touchdown. Jon Arnett had a 2-yard touchdown run. Leclerc kicked the extra points.

In 1968, Sayers had a devastating knee injury. Brian Piccolo encouraged Sayers through a successful rehabilitation. In 1969, Sayers led the league in rushing and Piccolo got cancer.

Sayers received the George Halas Award for Courage. In a speech that my father, Ed McCaskey, wrote for Sayers, Gale gave the award to Brian.

In 1977, my grandfather, George Halas, presented Sayers for induction into the Pro Football Hall of Fame. Here is part of the speech that my father wrote for my grandfather.

"Today I tell you that if you would see perfection at running back you had best get a film of Gale Sayers. He was poetry in motion and we shall never see his like again."

A Lifelong Learner

When I was a student
At Saint Mary's School
In Des Plaines,
The City of Destiny,
I learned that
Prayer is a spiritual telephone.

Now, I go
To Saint Mary's Church
In Lake Forest,
The City of Trees.
I propose that
Confession is a spiritual haircut.

Let's Continue to Help Each Other Get to Heaven

When I was on the search committee for a new school president for Notre Dame Prep, I asked candidate Ralph Elwart,

"What's your Confirmation name?"

He replied, "Samuel, after Cardinal Samuel Stritch."
Cardinal Stritch broke ground for Notre Dame High School.
The Holy Cross Congregation has had a continual presence at Notre Dame College Prep because of Father Conyers. He said Mass for us so we invited him to our 50 Year Anniversary dinner.

Freshman Year

When we were freshmen, Mister Wicklund taught us that swear words were clichés. We should express ourselves with fresh language.

Sophomore Year

When we were sophomores, A. J. Kozole was the sophomore basketball coach. I was on my way to basketball practice and Father Sandonato stopped me. He said, *"McCaskey, you have a unique writing talent. You should develop it."*

I replied, *"Father, I have to get to practice."*

We were a very good team until Steve Orser was brought up to the varsity. We were a very good team again when John Egart and Jimmy McCauley were brought up from the freshman team.

I didn't start against Glenbrook North, but I fouled out before the half. Now I shoot free throws until I make ten.

Junior Year

When we were juniors, we learned United States History from Dennis Roach. He taught us that the Gettysburg Address was a two and half-minute speech. The man who talked before Abraham Lincoln talked for two hours and nobody remembers what he said.

Senior Year

When we were seniors, the football team was 9–0 and conference co-champions. The track team was 10–1 and conference champions.

We survived the Great Snowstorm of 1967. On January 26, it started at 5:00 a.m. There were 23 inches of snow in the

PATRICK MCCASKEY AT NOTRE DAME

next 29 hours. Winds blew at 53 miles per hour. I was working out with the distance runners in the school parking lot that afternoon. Finally, the coach, Father Phil Devlin, said, "All right, you can go in now."

Now I'm running masters track. Masters is for people over thirty, which we are.

The snow melted in time for the Jugglers' musical, "Funny Girl."[94]

After we had our Senior Prom at the Edgewater Beach Hotel, it had to be demolished. Maybe it was just coincidental.

Weather is a reminder that God is The Boss. Mark Twain said, *"I have the calm, quiet confidence of a Christian with four aces."*

I prayed with confidence that there would be no snow for our 50 year reunion.

Notre Dame High School Class of 1967, let's continue to help each other get to heaven.

BOBBY WATKINS

In New Bedford, Massachusetts, Mayor Jon Mitchell, the school committee, and the city council wanted to improve the high school sports facility and they wanted to name it after someone appropriate. According to Mitchell, one name came to mind right away—Bobby Watkins.

Watkins is regarded as someone who has lived the kind of life that kids should aspire to live. Watkins graduated from New Bedford High School in 1951 and he was a standout athlete who went on to set numerous records on the football grid-iron at Ohio State where he played for Woody Hayes.

Bobby Watkins was a 2nd round draft choice of the Chicago Bears in 1955. He played running back for the Bears from 1955 through 1957. He is a Civil War expert. At the request of the good people of New Bedford, Massachusetts, here is my statement about him:

Three score and 2 years ago the Chicago Bears drafted Bobby Watkins in the second round. Now the Bobby Watkins Sports Facility will be in his hometown of New Bedford, Massachusetts. It is altogether fitting and proper that this should be done.

SPORTS, FAITH, AND SEATING

When I was a student at Saint Mary's School in Des Plaines, the City of Destiny, the teachers usually seated the students in alphabetical order. Sometimes, students who misbehaved were placed next to students who behaved. Don Nevins often sat next to me. He is now an excellent priest. He is pastor of Saint Agnes of Bohemia in Chicago.

When Don was a student at Saint Mary of the Lake Seminary in Mundelein, the teachers usually seated the students in alphabetical order. Sometimes, students who misbehaved were placed next to students who behaved. Jerry Listecki often sat next to Don Nevins. Jerry Listecki is now an excellent archbishop. He is doing Bears' missionary work in the Milwaukee archdiocese.

On Sunday, November 12, as I write this, the Chicago Bears are about to play the Green Bay Packers at Soldier Field. Here is my message:

Bears and Packers love your enemies, live the Gospel, let sportsmanship prevail, help each other get to Heaven: wheat and chaff.

MY BEST GAME

There have been just a few requests for a description of my best game, but here it is anyway. On Friday, October 21, 1966, Notre Dame High School played Saint Edward's High School in football at Notre Dame. Notre Dame Halfbacks Tom Newton, Owen Bauler, and Gary Aylesworth were hurt. So we had to pass more.

It was cold and windy. In the first and third quarters, we drove from the south to the north. The wind was at our backs. I was defensive signal caller, right outside linebacker, and quarterback for Notre Dame.

OFFENSE	DEFENSE
87 E Ken Powers	73 E Bob Rammon
77 T Pete Newell	54 T Mike Shaw
66 G Dick Ryglowski	77 T Pete Newell
54 C Mike Shaw	71 E Rick Rammon
61 G Bill Marquardt	80 LB Joe Petricca
74 T Jerry Jasinski	87 LB Ken Powers
83 E Frank Urban	52 LB Kevin Murninghan
10 QB Pat McCaskey	10 LB Pat McCaskey
23 HB Kevin Host	21 HB Mike Newton
21 HB Mike Newton	34 HB Pat Hughes
44 FB Greg Luzinski	85 S Bob Feltz
20 K Steve Hurley	44 P Greg Luzinski

In the first quarter, on fourth and one, Saint Ed's didn't make the first down. Notre Dame took over on the Saint Ed's 33. Notre Dame fumbled and Saint Ed's recovered. Then they punted.

Notre Dame Fullback Greg Luzinski ran for four yards. Then I dropped back and completed a 15-yard pass to him over the middle. Right halfback Mike Newton ran 20 yards to the 11.

Then we ran belly option 8 pass. Host went in motion to the right. I faked a handoff to Luzinski off right tackle Jerry

Jasinski, rolled right, and threw an 11-yard touchdown pass to Newton. Steve Hurley kicked the extra point.

Hurley kicked off into the end zone. Saint Ed's drove for a first down. Then left outside linebacker Joe Petricca and left defensive left halfback Mike Newton forced the Saint Ed's quarterback to fumble. Defensive left end Bob Rammon recovered the ball on the Saint Ed's 25. Luzinski ran for 6 yards.

Then we ran belly option 8 pass again. Host went in motion to the right. I faked a handoff to Luzinski off Jasinski, rolled right, and threw a 19-yard touchdown pass to Newton. Hurley kicked the extra point.

In the second quarter, Saint Ed's drove 54 yards for a touchdown and extra point. Fullback Ted Ewart scored both on short runs. Notre Dame had a 30-yard drive, but then fumbled.

In the third quarter, we ran belly option 8 pass again. Host went in motion to the right. I faked a handoff to Luzinski off Jasinski, rolled right, and threw a 43-yard touchdown pass to Newton. Hurley kicked the extra point.

One drive later, we ran belly option 8 pass again. Host went in motion to the right. I faked to Luzinski off Jasinski and rolled right. Everyone was covered; so I threw the ball out of the end zone.

At the end of the next drive, a play came in from the bench. Make it look like belly option 8 pass, but I should run. Host went in motion to the right. I faked to Luzinski off Jasinski, rolled right, faked a pass to Newton, and ran 24 yards for a touchdown. Hurley kicked the extra point.

Bob Rammon blocked a punt. Luzinski recovered it and ran three yards for a touchdown. Hurley kicked the extra point.

Newton ran 12 yards for a touchdown. Hurley kicked the extra point.

In the fourth quarter, Mark Havlis ran 18 yards for a touchdown. Hurley kicked the extra point.

Notre Dame won 49–7. Hurley set a school record for extra points (7) and longest kickoff (65). Newton tied the school record for touchdown receptions (3). Shaw had 18 tackles; Rick Rammon had 16; Powers had 15; Murninghan had 11; and Bob Rammon had 11.

I completed 5 of 6 for 94 yards and 3 touchdowns. I had 4 carries for 36 yards and 1 touchdown. I made 5 tackles.

Here's what John McCarthy wrote for the October 27, 1966, "Pickwick Newspapers." "Notre Dame completely dominated the third quarter, rolling up 28 points in the 12-minute span. This was the real Notre Dame; they were an animal-like machine, ferocious but with perfect precision."

PAT SIMEK MANNO

Pat Simek Manno grew up on Vassar Lane in the Cumberland section of Des Plaines. She went to Saint Mary's School. From the eighth grade yearbook, we know that her pet peeve was washing dishes. Her ambition was to be a nurse. She willed her torn up shoelace to Tom Jensen. It was predicted that she would be an astronaut. She was not a loud mouth. She was blonde. At the eighth grade party in the school hall, she was in the scarecrow dance.

From the 25-year reunion booklet, we know that she was a mother, housewife, and student at Harper College. She was in her second year working on a degree in Special Education. She was a graduate of the School of Cosmetology. She and her husband, Ron, had four children–Nicole, Cory, Mario, and Kyle.

Her worst job was at an insurance company; it was boring. Her best job was at Armand's Beauty Salon; she was a hairdresser. It was a fun job because there was a lot of people contact. Her favorite grade school memory was graduation. She was happy to be graduating and was proud to be part of the class of 1963.

Her best experience since grade school was giving birth to her gorgeous children. Her message or thought to share was *"let's not forget two special people. Ken Okon who had to leave us suddenly, and Sister Arthesma, who helped us through our grief. She was a special lady. For those of you who didn't know, she was at our graduation. She was sitting in a wheelchair in the choir watching us graduate."*

Two of Pat's sons, Mario and Kyle, were often with her at our class reunions. Kyle is now a priest. Her funeral was Tuesday, October 24, 2017, at Saint Thomas the Apostle Church in Crystal Lake, Illinois. Mario was a pallbearer. Kyle was the celebrant.

Proverbs 31:31 was on the first page of the program. *"Give her the reward she has earned, and let her works bring her praise at the city gate."*

FATHER MANNO'S BAPTISM SHIRT

FATHER KYLE MANNO

In Palatine, Illinois, Father Kyle Manno grew up the youngest of four children of two loving parents, Pat and Ron. At Northern Illinois University, he studied music education. During his time in college, he took sign language classes from a priest at a local parish that led to his vocation discernment. After graduation from Northern Illinois University and much prayer, he decided to apply to the seminary. He was accepted at Mundelein where he studied philosophy for 2 years and theology for 4 more. During his time in seminary, he was able to study Spanish in Mexico, as well as in El Salvador while working at an orphanage with 250 kids.

On June 5, 2016, Father Manno was ordained to the priesthood and he now serves at Christ the Teacher Parish in DeKalb, Illinois, and he is the Director of the Rockford Illinois Diocesan Vocation Office. Working hard to evangelize, Father Manno makes use of his musical talents. His famous video spoof of Carpool Karaoke that he created with Father Keith Romke (who is Pastor at Saint Patrick in Dixon) and Bishop David Malloy of Rockford, has "gone viral."[95] Father Manno wants to help Catholics experience their faith as joyful and engaging. He wants people to go to heaven. If Carpool Karaoke can help accomplish this, he is all in.

ABOUT HIS VOCATION

"I can honestly say, that [my ordination] was the happiest day of my life. I cannot imagine doing anything else. I am so excited to be here (his parish at the time) and I want all of you to know that you can contact me for anything you need. Never think that I am too busy, because the priesthood of Jesus Christ and my life is not about me, it's about the people of God. As a deacon, I was ordained to serve. As a priest, I was ordained to give up my life so that all of you can get to heaven…"

SAINT MARY'S ALL SCHOOL REUNION

As a tribute to Father Patrick Bird, who was our Pastor at Saint Mary's Church, we looked behind us and picked up all our belongings. Then we genuflected on the right knee.

After Mass on First Fridays, we were allowed to stand at tables and eat breakfast with hot chocolate that cost 10 cents a cup. The proceeds went to the missions. We were also allowed to buy candy at lunchtime in that hall. The proceeds went to the missions.

We saw many good movies in that hall for 10 cents that went to the missions. We saw "The Bells of Saint Mary's," "The Glenn Miller Story," "The Pride of the Yankees," "The Spirit of Saint Louis," and "The Student Prince."

I don't have Lou Gehrig's disease, but you say I have had a bad break because I am a speaker at this reunion. I admired

Gary Cooper as Lou Gehrig in the movie "Pride of the Yankees." Many of the words that follow are Lou Gehrig's via Gary Cooper and *Sports Illustrated*.

For the past several months you have been hearing about this reunion. I went to Saint Mary's School for 8 years, and I never received anything but kindness and encouragement from classmates. Look at the 1963 Saint Mary's School Championship Basketball Team. Which of you wouldn't consider it the highlight of his career just to associate with them for even one day? Sure I'm lucky. Who wouldn't consider it an honor to have known Father Buhrfiend and Father Grace? Also, the builder of Saint Mary's Parish Father Bird? To have spent many years with that wonderful fellow Father Maginot? Then to have spent 2 years with that outstanding leader, that smart student of psychology, the best coach in basketball, Bernie Delaney? Sure I'm lucky. When Saint Stephens School, a team you would give your right arm to beat, and vice versa, does not wreck this reunion—that's something. When you have a father and mother who work all their lives so that you can have an education and build your body—it's a blessing. When you have a wife who has been a tower of strength—that's the finest I know. People say that I've had a bad break. But today, today I consider myself the luckiest man on the face of the earth.

Rule of Saint Benedict

The Rule of Saint Benedict has been a fundamental guide for monastic life for many centuries. Saint Benedict of Nursia lived around 500 AD and *Saint Benedict's Rule* has since served as a guide for those who wanted to live in community and in faith. The term "ora et labora" (pray and work) describes the Benedictine way in a nutshell. *Saint Benedict's Rule* encourages community members to avoid idleness and directs them to spend their time in prayer, labor, and sacred reading. *The Rule* advocates a balance in life that keeps people on task. Of course, many Christians keep busy outside of monasteries. We are not all meant to be monks, ministers, or other Religious, but we can forge a life of prayer and labor. Many of the best in sport have done just that.

Saint Patrick

There is a huge volume of material both written and oral on the great Saint. But the actual material written about him by him is quite small. The *Confessio,* his spiritual autobiography, and the *Epistola* (or Letter) to Coroticus are the two documents or hard evidence that we have on him. Many look at the *Confessio* and the *Epistola* for a starting point, but at the same time, we do not dismiss tradition. Much of the traditional aspects of Saint Patrick are important, but the authoritative materials give us a view of the man that we should not ignore.

In the United States, we have made a kind of cartoon out of St. Patrick because we were using a neon St. Patrick to give us all a sense of identity and pride. We overloaded the holy day with a lot of Holiday hijinks like we Americans seem to do with our most important days. The commercialism associated with St. Patrick can blind us from the true man and saint.

St. Patrick lived in the 5th century. He was taken from his home by Irish pirates in an area of Britain (many say part of the future Scotland, some Wales) at age 16 and journeyed to what we call Ireland today as a slave. His captors released the young boy to look after some animals as a shepherd. But he lived in fear. He was left on his own to take care of the animals for long periods of time. By his own account, Patrick's faith was weak, although his father was a deacon and his grandfather a priest. Alone with his thoughts, he turned to prayer for comfort and protection. He became good at it. His faith grew strong on the lonely fields. After 6 years, he was inspired to escape and after a dangerous journey he found his way back home.

Patrick was very humble—anything, but proud. He took up his studies to become a priest, but had feelings of insecurity. Perhaps his best learning years had been taken up in slavery and it must have been a tough road to the priesthood. Later, he would become a Bishop.

Inspired to go back to Ireland and spread the faith, Patrick returned to the real possibility of death. Although fearful, he went back with courage and was successful in converting both royalty and commoners. Scholars suggest that the conversion of Ireland was hardly a one-man show, but most believe Patrick played a major part. Writers have noted that the conversion was peaceful.

The faithful and humble man that was Saint Patrick hardly reflects the holiday hero that many drink to today.

However, many people possess a rich sense of the Saint from any number of stories, songs, and writings. Saint Patrick's Breastplate or his Lorica surfaced a long time after his death. It has the desperate voice of a human being who had St. Patrick's fears and his constant need of God's protection. It is a beautiful prayer or chant. Like his life itself, the prayer speaks to those of us today who see and seek divine strength and intervention in daily life.

A small part of the prayer follows:

I arise today
Through the strength of heaven:
Light of sun
Radiance of moon
Splendor of fire
Speed of lightning
Swiftness of wind
Depth of sea
Stability of earth
Firmness of rock.
I arise today
Through God's strength to pilot me:
God's might to uphold me,
God's wisdom to guide me
God's eye to look before me,
God's ear to hear me,
God's word to speak for me,
God's hand to guard me,
God's way to lie before me,
God's host to save me
From snares of devils
From temptations of vices
From everyone who shall wish me ill,
Afar and anear,
Alone and in a multitude.[96]

QUIZ—QUARTERBACKS

Questions

1. Which sixth round draft pick from the University of Michigan made all the difference in the world to his pro team, his coach, and the team owner?

2. Which recent NFL quarterback won Super Bowls for two different "horsey" teams? His brother and father have played QB as well.

3. Who was the Monongahela, Pennsylvania, native who led his team to 4 Super Bowl wins and won 3 Super Bowl MVPs?

4. Which Golden Arm Quarterback cut by the Steelers played for 17 seasons with the Baltimore Colts and was voted NFL Player of the Year three times?

5. In 17 seasons in Miami, which quarterback rewrote practically every record in passing in the NFL record book?

6. From 1983 through 1998, which quarterback dressed in orange and led his team to five victories in six AFC championship games and two Super Bowl wins?

7. Which quarterback from Gulfport, Mississippi, played for 20 seasons and led his team to one Super Bowl Victory? He passed for 508 regular season touchdowns.

8. Which quarterback from Louisiana has been a regular on television, an actor, singer, book author and has received his own star on the Hollywood Walk of Fame? He also

led his team to 4 Super Bowl wins!

9. Recipient of several man of the year awards, which quarterback from Texas also holds the record for the all-time leader in completion percentage?

10. Which California-born quarterback has career pass ratings that are though the roof? One of today's (2018) best.

Answers

1. Tom Brady
2. Peyton Manning
3. Joe Montana
4. Johnny Unitas
5. Dan Marino
6. John Elway
7. Brett Favre
8. Terry Bradshaw
9. Drew Brees
10. Aaron Rodgers

Faith Poems

Introduction

In this final chapter of *Worthwhile Struggle* I have included some of my poems. I am a lector at the Church of Saint Mary and Saint Patrick Church in Lake Forest where some of these poems are read. Others are read at my presentations to churches, schools, and faith-based organizations of all kinds.

MATTHEW

CHRIST TAUGHT BEFORE HE PERFORMED MIRACLES

Matthew 5:1-12

From the Navarre Bible commentary,
We know that, "The Beatitudes proclaim
How to be fortunate, blessed." Jesus
Christ sustains hope in the midst of our trials.

The meek "do not give in to bitterness."
The merciful overlook faults and help out.
The peacemakers have inner peace and get
Themselves and others reconciled to God.

The Sermon on the Mount took fifteen min-
utes. I wasn't there, but I have typed it
And timed it because I wanted to know
How long it took for the greatest sermon.

Living the Beatitudes is as easy
As an eight-step handshake. Let's demonstrate.

Jesus Went and Told It on a Mountain

Matthew 5:1-12

The Beatitudes begin like the Psalms.
Christ said God was constant and generous.
It's a small world; so we have to behave.
It's for us to help mend what is broken.

Even on Earth, meekness is not weakness.
Jackie Vernon said, "Meek shall inherit
The earth. They'd be too scared to refuse it."

When we think about the poor in spirit,
The mourners, the meek, the righteous seeking,
The merciful, the heart clean, peacemakers,
And the persecuted, let's remember
Boy Scouts are trustworthy, loyal, helpful,
Friendly, courteous, kind, obedient,
Cheerful, thrifty, brave, clean, and reverent.

Upright Intention throughout the Nation

Matthew 6:1-6, 16-18

From the Navarre Bible commentary,
We know that, Jesus Christ "teaches that true
Devotion calls for sincerity and
A right intention, intimacy with
God without parading one's piety."

I've already given up alcohol,
Candy, desserts, sodas, and tobacco.

Many years ago, maybe last century,
Cardinal George wrote a column in the
"Catholic New World" about giving up
Resentments for Lent. It is altogether
Fitting and proper that I should do this.

For each Lent, self-denial is back in style.
If we do our best, God will do the rest.

Following Jesus Christ Is Not Easy

Matthew 8:18-22

From the Navarre Bible commentary,
We know that Christ "acts with authority."

A scribe said that Jesus was a teacher.
Jesus said that He did not have a home.
A disciple saw Christ as a preacher.
The scribe could have written Him a poem.

True disciples follow Christ all the time.
"Nothing is more important than" heaven.
The Son of man had the ultimate plan.
Follow Him since He was the Son of God.

Remember an eighth grade basketball cheer.
One, two, three, four, five, six, seven, all good
Players go to heaven. When they get there,
They repeat. Saint Mary's cannot be beat.

JESUS RAISED A GIRL AND CURED A WOMAN

Matthew 9:18-26

After the daughter of a ruler had
Died, he humbled himself before Jesus.
Jesus said she was not dead, but sleeping.
After the laughter, He raised her to life.

A woman had suffered for twelve years, but
She believed in Jesus. If she could touch
His garment, she would be cured. She was right.

We get to receive Communion each day.
All we have to do is humble ourselves.
Then our faith in Christ will be rewarded.
When we need healing, show faith in Jesus.

Father Michael Nacius anointed me.
On June 13, I had surgery for
Prostate cancer. The surgery went quite
Well. I'm off the catheter and prune juice.

GOD SENT THE APOSTLES ON A MISSION

Matthew 10:7-13

From the Navarre Bible commentary,
We know that, "Jesus is training his twelve
Apostles for their mission, which" the Church
Continues until The Second Coming.

Jesus said that God's Kingdom had come.
That was the message of the apostles.
Jesus Christ performed many miracles.
The apostles went forth and did likewise.

Christ was detached from material things.
The apostles were to imitate Christ.
Jesus gave them a sense of urgency
To give up worrying about their needs.

Jesus gave the apostles the treasure
Of peace. They gave peace when they were welcomed.

DISCIPLESHIP HAS DEMANDS AND REWARDS

Matthew 10:37-42

Jesus before your father or mother.
Jesus before your sister or brother.
To be Jesus worthy take up His cross.
Do it always, even after a loss.

We can find Jesus through the narrow gate.
When we go to Mass, let us not be late.
If we take up the cross, we will find life.
Let us forget ourselves, even in strife.

Our reward is heavenly reception.
We will be received without deception.
Prophets and the righteous received rewards.
They are pointed heaven towards.

Let us have a cold water cup to drink.
Disciples and children teach us to think.

THREE PARABLES SHOW THE WAY TO HEAVEN

Matthew 13:24-43

Seeds and weeds are grown together on Earth.
On the last day, seeds will have a rebirth.
Weeds will be burned; they are not heaven sent.
The condemned will have a permanent Lent.

A tiny mustard seed starts out quite small.
The seed grows more than Bill Wennington tall.
A bird can settle in a tree and nest.
When the Bulls are playing, Bill does not rest.

Children grow and grow like bread from some yeast.
Let's hope they learn to take care of the least.
Our bread order was sixteen loaves a week.
As we live each day, it's fine to be meek.

Right here on Earth we have both wheat and chaff.
Let's love each other and have a good laugh.

A Woman Has a Debate with Jesus

Matthew 15:21-28

A woman asked Christ to heal her daughter
Who was possessed on her way to slaughter.
At first, Christ did not answer the woman.
The apostles asked to send her away.

Jesus said, "I was sent for the lost sheep."
The woman then asked for help again.
Jesus said, "Children's food is not for dogs."
The woman replied, "The dogs eat the scraps."

Jesus said, "O woman great is your faith!"
Then he cured her daughter at that hour.
What can we learn from these humble verses?
When we ask for help, do not use curses.

All the lost sheep need help that is divine.
Jesus provides it, if we do not whine.

CHAIR OF SAINT PETER THE APOSTLE

Matthew 16:13-19

Right after Peter had confessed his faith,
Jesus gave him the keys to the Kingdom.
Pete was promised his future primacy.
He said Christ was Messiah and God's Son.

We can make this profession too, through faith.
God gave Peter and us the gift of faith.
Christ made Peter the leader of the Church.
Peter was the Apostles' quarterback.

Saints have seen Popes as Peter's successors.
Bears have also seen this Papal vision.
Peter has the Kingdom keys; we have fobs.
Those of us in Legatus have great jobs.

Legatus is Latin: ambassador.
We drive in the far right lane for Jesus.[97]

TRANSFIGURATION

Matthew 17: 1-9

We can never know the Second Coming date
But we think about it anyway
And we wonder if we're really with God now
Or just praying after some finer day

Transfiguration
Transfiguration
Is making us great
Is keeping us waiting

And we tell God how easy it is to be with Him
And how right His arms feel around us
But, I wrote this poem just yesterday
When I was thinking about how right this Mass might be

Transfiguration
Transfiguration
Is making us great
Is keeping us waiting

And after Mass we can have more fellowship
We can win championships with sportsmanship
So we'll try and see into God's eyes right now
And just pray right here
Since Jesus died for our sins

Jesus died for our sins
And pray right here
Since Jesus died for our sins
Jesus died for our sins
Jesus died for our sins[98]

A Tale of Two Sons: A Lesson for All

Matthew 21: 28-32

Two sons struggled to do their father's will.
One son said no to work; then he did work.
The other said yes and then he did not.
Blazing Saddles' Mel Brooks said, "work, work, work."

Work is a blessing that we should not shirk.
Not only do it, but do it with heart.
At the office, my father used to say,
"Work is the thing that makes our hearts sing."

The tax collectors and the prostitutes
Saw John the Baptist come in righteousness.
They believed in him and they repented.
They applied for heaven; God relented.

Appearances don't fool God Almighty.
Be authentic; work with integrity.

THE PARABLE OF THE MARRIAGE FEAST

Matthew 22:1-14

Jesus was a master storyteller.
A king gave a wedding feast for his son.
The bride and the groom were not registered.
There was not a rehearsal dinner.

The invited guests did not attend.
After they were invited again, they
Killed the servants who had invited them.
The king killed the killers and burned their city.

The king sent his servants to invite others.
Good people and bad people accepted.
When the king saw one who was not wearing
A wedding garment, the king removed him.

This was not the wedding of the century.
Thank God for the wedding feast at Cana.

Preparation for the Day of Judgment

Matthew 25:1-13

Jesus told us about the ten virgins.
"Five of them were foolish and five were wise."
The foolish ones did not bring oil with them.
The wise ones brought flasks of oil for their lamps.

While they waited all of them fell asleep.
They were awakened to meet the bridegroom.
The foolish ones asked the wise ones for oil.
The wise ones sent the foolish to the store.

The foolish ones went to buy enough oil.
The wise ones and the bridegroom went inside.
By the time the foolish ones were prepared,
It was too late. The foolish were locked out.

Like mature Boy Scouts, let us be prepared.
My father said, "Be alert at all times."

CHRIST AROSE AND APPEARED TO THE WOMEN

Matthew 28:8-15

Jesus first appeared to holy women
Because they had been faithful and valiant.
Then Jesus appeared to the apostles.
He had not seen them since the Last Supper.

Matthew avoids giving minor details.
The Resurrection was magnificent.
It was extraordinary.
Easter Sunday is a Hall of Fame day.

The soldiers who were stationed at the Tomb
Were given bribes to say that the body
Of Jesus had been stolen. Matthew wrote
In glorious, humble disagreement.

Soldiers of Christ do not take bribes, but we're
Allowed to accept Confirmation gifts.

MARK

ISAIAH THE PROPHET; JOHN THE BAPTIST

Mark 1:1-8

Isaiah the prophet was a writer
Who was smart enough to let God use him.
He was an Old Testament advance man.
He told us all about John the Baptist.
John was the New Testament advance man.
He told us to repent for forgiveness.

John the Baptist was not a real fun guy.
He was not mellow; he could sure bellow.
He called everyone a brood of vipers.
He would have sent Boy Scouts looking for snipes.
Instead of loaves and fishes, he ate locusts.
He was not a listener; we listen.

We hear him say, "Jesus is mightier."
Let's be grateful for Isaiah and John.

CHRIST WAS TEMPTED BEFORE HIS MINISTRY

Mark 1:12-15

After Jesus was baptized, he fasted.
He did not have any cake or ice cream.
The Spirit drove Jesus to the desert,
Before the Raiders moved to Las Vegas.

The temptation shows the humanity
Of Jesus. He did not yield to Satan.
The angels ministered to Jesus Christ.
He did not lord his greatness over them.

If we want God's Kingdom, we must repent.
Every day is Christmas; each day is Lent.
Repentance and belief saved the good thief.
Reconciliation leads to salvation.

After Satan provided temptation,
Jesus gave us Gospel proclamation.

THE LEPROSY LEFT HIM; HE WAS MADE CLEAN

Mark 1:40-45

From the Navarre Bible commentary,
We know that, "In the gestures and words of
This leper seeking a cure from Jesus,
We can see his prayer (which is full of faith),
And his delight once he is cured…Jesus'
Own gestures and words show his compassion…"

After I had graduated from high school,
The Pat McCaskey Award was started.
It went to that member of the track team,
Who had the most acne on his back.

Fourteen years ago, cancer, basil cell
Carcinoma, was removed from my back.
It wasn't the curing of a leper,
But it was a helpful cure for cancer.

Jesus Did the Right Thing on the Sabbath

Mark 3:1-6

After Jesus had entered the temple,
He saw a man with quite a withered hand.
The denigrators and the second guessers
Were hoping Jesus would make a mistake.

Christ talked to the man and asked a question.
The silence of the Pharisees was not consent.
After Jesus had cured the withered hand,
The Pharisees worked hard on the Sabbath.

At the Mass we honored Saint Anthony.[99]
Tony lived by himself in the desert,
Since he did not know about Walden Pond.
He prayed and fasted except on Sundays.

Like Jesus and Saint Anthony, let us
Always strive and thrive to do the right thing.

JESUS CHRIST STRESSES PURITY OF HEART

Mark 7:1-8, 14-15, 21-23

From the "Workbook for Lectors" we know that,
"Jesus prefers to associate with
an amiable, if somewhat un-
tidy, Group rather than…critics with clean hands."

Jesus declared that all food is clean.
Sin begins in the interior life.
Jesus healed with just one look of true love.
Bing Crosby sang "True Love" to Grace Kelly.

God restores our heart with a tender gaze.
We can do the same the rest of our days.
Husbands can give their wives the look of love.
Parents can look at their children with love.

Jesus Christ looks at us with compassion,
Even if we do not like poetry.

THE CURING OF AN EPILEPTIC BOY

Mark 9:14-29

When Jesus and Peter and James and John
Came down from a high mountain, they came to
The other disciples and a great crowd.
When the crowd saw Jesus, they were amazed.

The father of an epileptic boy
Asked Christ to stop the seizures of his son.
The disciples were not able to help.
Christ invites the father to pray with faith.

Then Christ taught the disciples in private.
After His ascension, they had to pray.
Through the curing of an epileptic,
Christ teaches us to pray with confidence.

Mark Twain said, "I have the calm, quiet confidence of a Christian, with four aces."

INDISSOLUBILITY OF MARRIAGE

Mark 10:2-16

From the beginning, we're male and female.
A lineup like that does not become stale.
Saint John Paul II said married couples are
Called to "total mutual self-giving."

From the lectors' workbook, we know that, "lifelong monogamous marriage is the ideal."
Here's a slight "Young Frankenstein" rewrite, "Fidelity, no escaping that for me."

From the Navarre Bible commentary,
We know that, "the Kingdom of heaven be-
longs to those who receive it like a child."
We don't merit it. We accept God's gift.

Let's believe like children, love like children,
Abandon like children, pray like children.

A Rich Young Man Says No to Poverty

Mark 10:17-27

Christ called a rich young man to follow Him.
Unlike the first disciples, he said no.
Material things can become false gods.
When we know and love God, we can say yes.

It's important to keep a low profile.
I have the least expensive Cadillac.

My goal is to keep the Bears in the family until The Second Coming. In
the meantime, I shall continue to tithe.

The Parable of the Wicked Tenants

Mark 12:1-12

Jesus Christ was a great storyteller.
From the Navarre Bible commentary,
We know that, "In this parable Jesus
Provides a summary of salvation
History and of his own life and work."

God wants his Chosen People to be good.
There have been times when we were reluctant.
The servants are symbols of the prophets.
The son who was killed represents Jesus.

Like Old Testament Joseph who was not
Bitter to his brothers who had sold him,
Jesus tells this story without rancor.
It is all part of God's wonderful plan.

Jesus Christ started the excellent Church.
Through the Spirit, we're not left in the lurch.

Poem from a Former Patrol Boy

Mark 13:33-37

Jesus said that we should be vigilant.
From "Navarre" we know that we must be vibrant.
This is a parable; let's be prepared.
It is not good for us to know the time,
Since we would only be good at the end.
Being faithful is our mountain to climb.

Jesus is the traveling householder.
Peter is the vigilant gatekeeper.
We're the servants who are here to wash feet.
Getting to heaven would be really neat.
Our job is to obey the Commandments
In the spirit of the Beatitudes.

We are the sentinels and the sentries.
Like patrol boys, let us be attentive.

LUKE

Annunciation and Incarnation

Luke 1:26-38

Nazareth was not mentioned in the Old
Testament. But that is where the Angel
Gabriel announced to Mary that she
Would be the mother of Jesus, God's Son.

The Son of God would become human with-
out diminishing His divine nature.
Joseph and Mary were going steady.
The announcement helped Mary get ready.

The Old Testament is truly fulfilled.
Jesus Christ will have the throne of David.
Christ "will reign over the house of Jacob."
The Kingdom of Jesus will have no end.

Eve ate an apple; Mary was humble.
Eve disbelieved; Mary conceived Jesus.

MARY, THE IMMACULATE CONCEPTION

Luke 1:26-38

Gabriel wrote a prayer, the Hail Mary.
Nazareth was City of Destiny.
Joseph & Mary were obedient.
Then Gabriel said, "Do not be afraid."

Jesus descended from a king, David.
The Kingdom of Jesus will have no end.
Since Jesus was God's Son, He was holy.
Since Mary was God's Mom, she was holy.

Mary and Elizabeth were remarkable.
Like the Lone Ranger, Gabriel was gone.
Rodgers and Hammerstein's Cinderella sang,
"Impossible things are happening every day."

The WSFI anniversary:
All of you have been quite obedient.[100]

The Visitation; the Magnificat

Luke 1:39-56

Here is the Second Joyful Mystery.
Mary traveled to see Elizabeth
Who lived with her husband Zechariah.
She was quite pregnant with John the Baptist.

Elizabeth's words praised God and Mary.
Jesus would love even the contrary.
Mary would thank God for all He had done.
God the Father would even send His Son.

God shows mercy to each generation.
The Hail Mary is a great sensation.
Mary and her cousin had a visit.
Then Mary returned home, since she missed it.

The Magnificat was Mary's Praise Song.
At the All School Mass, let's all sing along.

THE SHEPHERDS FOUND THE HOLY FAMILY

Luke 2:16-21

The shepherds were nearby Israelites.
They went in haste to nearby Bethlehem.
They opened their hearts and received great joy.

Let us be grateful to the Apostles.
They replaced circumcision with Baptism.
Long before we are in an earthly tomb,
Now we can name babies in the womb.

When we are tempted to complain about
Accommodations, let us remember:
A stable was good enough for Jesus.

If we ever have one more flight delay,
We can still thank God for the Wright brothers.
If the Bears ever lose another game,
We can still be grateful for our mothers.

JESUS CAME TO ESTABLISH DIVISION

Luke 12:49-53

Our division is the NFC North.
We often play Lions, Packers, Vikings.
When you turn the other cheek, stand your ground.
Let's establish a solid running game.

Some attend every game; some do not.
Let there be amnesty for the no shows.
Jesus came to set the earth on fire.
We have read about the Chicago fire.

Jesus did not come to establish peace.
That's why football is a collision sport.
Some root for the Cubs; some root for the Sox.
The important thing is we're all Bear fans.

Jesus was here to divide households.
Thank God for homilies to explain why.
We must follow the voice of Jesus Christ
From conception to a natural death.

Feast Day of Saint Margaret of Scotland

Luke 17:20-25

Jesus said the Kingdom of God is here.
It was not observed; it was not announced.
Jesus told His disciples to stay put.
"Do not go off, do not run in pursuit."

Jesus said He had to suffer greatly.
Then He would be like lightning in the sky.
His generation would soon reject Him.
On Easter He would triumph by and by.

Saint Margaret of Scotland was saintly.[101]
She founded monasteries and churches.
She diligently took care of the poor.
She brought travelers to Saint Andrew's shrine.

Andrew was an original Apostle.
He saw Jesus as lightning in the sky.

JOHN

John the Baptist Leads Us to Jesus Christ

John 1:6-8, 19-28

God sent John to give us testimony.
John's testimony was not a phony.
The Baptist did not say he was the one.
He told us about Christ Who was God's Son.

The questions for John were very many.
None of them were worth even a penny.
John was patient and did not obfuscate.
He was very clear, unlike Watergate.

John was not Christ, Elijah, or prophet.
He did not sell equipment for Moffett.
Isaiah had told us John would be here.
Repent for our sins and be of good cheer.

John was not worthy to untie sandals.
And yet he was not involved in scandals.[102]

JESUS ENCOUNTERS HIS FIRST FOLLOWERS

John 1:35-42

John the Baptist pointed his disciples
To Christ and said, "Behold, the Lamb of God."
The disciples did not want detention.
So, they were quickly quite obedient.

Christ turned and asked, "What are you looking for?"
Apostle John asked, "Where are you staying?"
Jesus said to them, "Come, and you will see."
It was a divine, human dialogue.

After Andrew had spent time with Jesus,
Andrew went and found his brother Simon.
Andrew said, "We have found the Messiah."
Then Andrew brought Simon to Jesus Christ.

Jesus Christ changed Simon's name to Cephas.
Cephas means Peter; he was Christ's vicar.

Feast of Saint Bartholomew-Nathanael

John 1:45-51

If the Apostles had played football,
They would have been a great team.
We don't know much about Bartholomew,
So he would have been a lineman.
Let's put him at left guard with the nickname Bart.

Philip found Bartholomew-Nathanael.
We don't know much about Philip either,
So he would have been a lineman too.
Let's put him at left tackle with the nickname Phil.

Since Bart said that Jesus was the Son of God,
Jesus said that Bart "will see heaven opened
And the angels of God ascending and
Descending on the Son of Man."
That would be a great postgame show.[103]

THE CURING OF A ROYAL OFFICIAL'S SON

John 4:43-54

A royal official traveled twenty
Miles from Capernaum to Cana to ask
Jesus to cure his son who was near death.
The official was humbly persistent.

The official wanted Jesus to go
To Capernaum. Jesus cured long distance.
Miracles call us to faith and belief.
They show God's mercy and mighty power.

When I was a high school junior, I rode
My bike twenty-five miles from Des Plaines to
Wheaton to see someone. She wasn't home.
Eighteen years later, I got married there.

My hair was brown, curly, and thick. Now my
Hair is white, straight, and thin.
God is protecting my marriage.
I was too good looking.

The Miracle of the Loaves and Fishes

John 6:1-15

From the "Workbook for Lectors," we know that,
A large crowd had seen Jesus help the sick.
He climbed a mountain with his disciples.
The crowd followed them with a great hunger.

Jesus asked Philip "how can we feed them?"
Philip did the accounting in despair.
Andrew told Christ about a boy with food.
Jesus had five thousand sit on the grass.

Christ multiplied five loaves and two fishes.
They had an excellent sufficiency.
Let this Gospel be a reminder. God
Performs miracles for people of faith.

When I was a child, the bread order for
My family was sixteen loaves a week.

Jesus Discoursed about the Bread of Life

John 6:22-29

After Jesus had multiplied loaves and
Fishes and walked on water, people looked
For Him. They had had an excellent suf-
ficiency. So, they wanted to thank Him.

Filled with food, they took boat rides to Christ.
This prefigured the calls at the
Billy Graham Crusades. "The busses will wait."
Jesus gave us faith and eternal life.

Jesus said to them, "Do not work for food
That perishes but for food that endures
For eternal life." We have Communion.
Catholics can have Communion every day.

Passover has become the Eucharist.
Instead of manna we have Communion.

The Bread of Life Is in the Eucharist

John 6:51-58

From the Lectors Workbook, we know that "John
the Evangelist is instructing us
about the value of the Eucharist.
It is offered…from the altar as bread and wine
transformed into the" Lamb's Body and Blood.

From the Navarre Bible commentary,
we know that, "Jesus…is inviting us
to partake often of His Body, as
nourishment for our souls," our daily bread.

Transubstantiation is wonderful.
We can eat and drink the Lamb's Flesh and Blood.
The Church is a halfway house to heaven.

Since exhumation is part of canonization, I do not want cremation.

Isaac Was Restored; Jesus Christ Arose

John 8:51-59

God told Abraham he would have a son.
After Isaac's birth, the work was not done.
God told Abraham: sacrifice Isaac.
Abraham agreed; he did not look back.

Right after the test, Isaac was restored.
When you work with God, you are never bored.
Abraham Isaac are quite a story.
They were righteous and worked for God's glory.

Christ died for our sins; He was quite the Man.
He arose from the dead: what a great plan.
After our earthly death, live forever.
We can live with God, leaving Him never.

Christ died for our sins, including fumbles.
With God in heaven, no one there mumbles.

THE CHURCH IS THE GATEWAY TO JESUS CHRIST

John 10:1-10

David was a shepherd who became a king.
Christ was a king who became a shepherd.
Jesus fulfilled the ancient prophecies
Of Jeremiah and Ezekiel.

The illustration of Jesus as the
Good Shepherd shows God's love for each of us.
Like the Waltons at bedtime, He calls all
Of us: "Good night Saint Mary's; follow Me."

Jesus speaks through the Church; let us listen
To the priests, the cardinals, and the pope.
If they say something that we do not like,
Let's not mope. It's the feast day of Saint George.[104]

Saint George slayed dragons and rescued maidens.
Let's be chivalrous and charitable.

JESUS CHRIST LAID DOWN HIS LIFE
FOR HIS SHEEP

John 10:11-18

The Church is a flock with human shepherds.
Jesus leads us and brings us to pasture.
He knows us and calls each of us by name.
We have birth names and Confirmation names.

Priests take care of their flocks willingly. They
Are wonderful examples for their flocks.
They want salvation for every human.
They provide us with Holy Communion.

When we are in trouble, they do not run.
There are times when they let us have some fun.
They do not want anyone to be lost.
Like Saint Ignatius, they don't count the cost.

Jesus Christ gave His life for everyone.
Jesus Christ is a Hall of Fame shepherd.

CHRIST ANNOUNCES HIS GLORIFICATION

John 12:20-33

From the Navarre Bible commentary,
We know that, "Jesus…is…a seed that" dies
"And thereby produces abundant fruit."
He was humbled; then He was glorified.

Every suffering and contradiction
Shares Christ's cross. We're redeemed and exalted.
When we die to ourselves without a thought
To our own comfort or desires and plans,
We're supernaturally effective.

Christ fell three times on the walk to His death.
I threw three interceptions in one game.
Jesus rose from the dead to His glory.
I made Catholic All-American.

Intimate Conversation with Jesus

John 14: 15-21

The Ten Commandments are not suggestions.
God showed the way. Let there be no questions.
We keep the Commandments; Jesus is loved.
The Commandments are kept; Satan is shoved.

With The Advocate, there are no small ways.
The Advocate will be with us always.
The public life of Jesus was three years.
When we're obedient, we hear His cheers.

Jesus is in The Father; He's in us.
We're all working together; so don't fuss.
Let's observe the Commandments all the time.
Love God always; that's our mountain to climb.

We love Jesus; we're loved by His Father.
The Spirit tells Satan not to bother.

The Advocate Teaches Us Everything

John 14:21-26

From the Navarre Bible commentary,
We know that, Jesus wants us to show our
Love for God through "generous and faithful
Self-giving" and obeying the commandments.

Jesus is our Advocate in heaven.
The Spirit is our Advocate on earth.
When we're disheartened, the Spirit lifts us.
Spirit gives us a preview of heaven.

Saint Paul said that "each of us is a temple
Of the Holy Spirit. The Trinity
Dwells in the soul of each person." Spirit
Helps us understand what Jesus Christ said.

Today is the feast day of Saint Pius V.[105]
He was known for his strict fasting and prayer.

Jesus Is the Vine; We Are the Branches

John 15:1-8

The night before Jesus died, He spoke well.
He is the vine; His Father grows the vine.
We receive tribulations and temptations.
They make us stronger; we serve God longer.

My earthly father once said to me, "It's
Up to you, but you're doing it all wrong."
Accountability, encouragement
Help us get pruned of our ungodliness.

When we are with Jesus Christ, we sin less,
We do holy works, and we help others.
Mass and the sacraments, Bible study,
And daily devotions keep us attuned.

The Holy Trinity helps us stay pruned.
When Christ is our vine, we are mighty fine.

THE FATHER LOVED JESUS; JESUS LOVES US

John 15:9-17

Brotherly love led Jesus to the cross.
Jesus proved His love for us on the cross.
Love inspires us to keep the commandments.
Love for Christ leads us to obedience.

From the Navarre Bible commentary,
We know that, Jesus Christ is our best friend.

After Christ had ascended to heaven,
Matthias became the twelfth Apostle.

From the book called, "Who's Who in the Bible,"
We know that, "There had to be twelve to cor-
respond to the twelve tribes of Israel."

If the Apostles had played football, they
Would have been a great team. Matthias, who
Replaced Judas, would have been the kicker.

The Holy Spirit Testifies to Christ

John 15:26-16:4

Christ revealed Himself through His miracles.
We accept Him; our sins are forgiven.

Jesus sends The Spirit who testifies.
The Spirit helps us understand Jesus.
Our hearts are opened; we don't "fall away."

Father created a wonderful world.
Christ died for our sins, including fumbles.
Holy Spirit is always there for us.

God the Father allowed His Son to die.
Jesus ascended and sent The Spirit.
The Holy Spirit consoles and comforts.
Trials have good purpose; let our faith be seen.

The Trinity has cooperation.
They don't misbehave like the three stooges.

JESUS PRAYED FOR THE APOSTLES AND US

John 17:11-19

Jesus Christ asked His Father to keep His
Apostles in His name for communion
With Him. Their unity would reflect the
Unity of the Blessed Trinity.

The Trinity reigns with mutual love
And self-giving. We can discover our
True selves only when we give ourselves.

Jesus invites us to receive God's love.
Be in the world without being worldly.
Jesus died for us and gave us true life.

Jesus prayed this at the Last Supper.
Knute Rockne said, "Win one for the Gipper."

Jesus Christ Wrote More than the Our Father

John 17:20-26

Christ taught us to pray with the Our Father.
In this passage, He teaches us again.
When we have struggles, let's depend on Christ.
We can suffer with confidence in Him.

Perhaps your suffering is poetry.
This poem will be over in a minute.

Thank you for listening. This is better
Than talking to myself. It's great to be
With you. Let us be Hall of Fame Legates.

From Scott Hahn, we know that family is
The first society. Like Pope Francis,
Let us celebrate the good of the Church.

The Passion and the Death of Jesus Christ

John 18:1-19:42

Those who arrested Jesus were in awe.
We should do God's will the way Jesus did.
Isaac and Jesus were obedient.
Before the chief priests, Jesus was transparent.

Jesus Christ forgave Peter's denials
Because Peter had a great repentance.
Jesus was grateful for John's faithfulness.
Thank God for the sacrament of Penance.

When Jesus was before Pilate, Christ did
Not say much. He was like Gary Cooper.
Jesus Christ was whipped and then crowned with thorns.
Then Pilate handed Christ over for death.

Jesus carried His cross to Calvary.
His side was pierced and His cup was finished.

After Breakfast, Jesus Asked Three Questions

John 21: 15-19

The disciples had fasted all night.
Their stomachs were probably very light.
Jesus helped them break their fast with breakfast.
Fried fishes were a wonderful repast.

Jesus asked Peter a question three times.
Peter replied to Jesus without chimes.
The mandate from Jesus was very clear.
Love and build the Church and be of good cheer.

Christ said to Peter who was not asleep,
"Feed my lambs, tend my sheep, and feed my sheep."
When Peter was young, he went anywhere.
When he was mature, he was Fred Astaire.

Jesus showed Peter choreography.
Jesus had said to Peter, "Follow Me."

Patrick McCaskey

EASTER POEMS

Here are some poems for the Easter Season.

THE EMPTY TOMB FULFILLED THE PROPHECIES

John 20:1-9

Mary Magdalene was first at the Tomb.
When Peter and John arrived at the Tomb,
John let Peter enter first because he
Was the elder. John had run faster; Peter
Might have told John to do some stretching.

From the Navarre Bible commentary,
We know that, "the empty tomb, the linen
Cloths, the napkin in a place by itself"
Were the evidence that Jesus arose.
Detective Columbo was not needed.

John saw and believed and Peter achieved.
Peter and John did not understand the
Scripture. They needed Bible Study.

STOP.

294

Jesus on the Cross Gave Us His Mother

John 19:25-27

When we call out the signals and our voice cracks,
When we dribble down court and punt the ball,
When we're late for practice because of JUG,
Let us remember, we have God's Mother.

When we lose a close game to a rival,
When we are not heard at a pep rally,
When we are cut from the sophomore team,
Let us remember, we have God's Mother.

When we don't pass the football physical,
When we nearly drown at swimming practice,
When we run track like a football player,
Let us remember, we have God's Mother.

When we make All-Area quarterback,
Let us remember, to thank God's Mother.

JESUS MAKES THE DEAF HEAR AND THE MUTE SPEAK

Mark 7:31-37

From the Navarre Bible commentary,
We know that, Christ "now works a miracle
Using gestures that symbolize the
Saving power of his human nature."

Jesus opens our ears to enable
Us "to hear and accept the word of God."
Christ told the people to be quiet about
The miracle, but they did not listen.

Last year, I had surgery to remove
Non-cancerous growth from my inner ear.
It was an opportunity to do
John Byner's impersonation of John
Wayne as a brain surgeon. John Byner said,
"We're gonna have to yank it outta there."

Doctor Micco said, "We will not yank it."
Now I can still hear and accept God's word.

WALKING, TALKING TO EMMAUS

Luke 24: 13-35

They were walking to Emmaus,
Seven miles from Jerusalem.
Then Jesus walked and talked with them,
But they did not recognize Him.

They walked and talked; they walked and talked.
Jesus was a great listener.
They talked about Christ crucified.
Women could not find His body.

After Jesus had heard them out,
He told them Christ had to suffer.
Then He would enter His glory.
So said Moses and the prophets.

Christ stayed with them in Emmaus.
He broke bread and then He disappeared.

Pro-Life Poems

In 1838, Henry Wadsworth Longfellow's poem, "A Psalm of
Life" was published. I have slightly rewritten it.

Let's March For Life

Let us not, in mournful numbers,
March for but an empty dream!
For the unborn are in slumbers
We're marching for a great team.

March for real! March in earnest!
And the grave is not our goal;
Dust thou art, to dust returnest
Was not spoken of the soul.

Not enjoyment, and not sorrow,
Is our destined end or way;
But to march, that each tomorrow
Find us farther than today.

Art is long, and Time is fleeting,
And our hearts, though stout and brave,
Still, like muffled drums are beating
Funeral marches to the grave.

In the world's broad field of battle,
In the bivouac of Life,
Be not like dumb, driven cattle!
Let's be heroes in the strife!

Trust in God Almighty pleasant!
The dead Past bury its dead!
March, - march in the living Present!
Heart within, and God o'erhead!

March for Life friends all remind us
We can make our lives sublime,
Marching forward leave behind us
Footprints on the streets of time.

Footprints, that perchance another,
Marching on city's streets main,
A forlorn, heartbroken mother,
Seeing, shall take heart again.

Let us, then, be up and doing,
With a heart for any fate;
Still achieving, still pursuing,
March for Life, anticipate.

This Pro-Life Poem was inspired by Alfred Tennyson's poem "The Charge of the Light Brigade."

THE MARCH OF THE PRO-LIFERS

One cold mile, one cold mile
One cold mile forward
Through the streets of Chicago
Marched the Pro-Lifers

"Faster, the Pro-Lifers!"
Were we bound for heaven?
As though the marchers knew
Jesus had saved them.
Ours not to march too slow,
Ours not to march for show
Ours but to march and glow
Through the streets of Chicago
Marched the Pro-Lifers.

Encouraged with good spirits,
Faster we marched and well,
Into post march stiffness;
Back to the Federal Plaza
Marched the Pro-Lifers.

Marched all our reserves bare,
March as we needed air
Surging the last block there,
Marching one mile
Spectators marveled.

Marched through car exhaust smoke
A course record we broke:
We know that life
Begins at conception
After death, heaven
Is a promotion
All the Pro-Lifers

We don't have a palace.
We don't march with malice.
We who had marched so well
Endure post march stiffness
Back at the Federal Plaza,
All who started finished
All the Pro-Lifers.

Now will we drink lemonade?
Oh, the strong march we made!
Spectators marveled.
Honor the march we made!
Honor the Brave Marchers-
Noble Pro-Lifers!

Pro Life Roses for Mothers' Day

Wonderful mother, thank you for life.
I'm even grateful when there is strife.
Each one of my cells has twenty-three
Of your chromosomes, lucky for me.

Wonderful mother, here is a poem.
We say our prayers in our faith based home.
It's the least we can do says my wife.
Wonderful mother, thank you for life.

Church on Mothers' Day is not extreme.
We get grace from a Being Supreme.
We give red roses on Mothers' Day.
Pro Life chases abortion away.

For family milk we need a cow.
Listen, MOM spelled upside down is WOW.

– End Notes –

1   Attendance is voluntary.

2   Taken from the Sisters of Charity web site at: https://www.bvmsisters. org/about-us/history/.

3   Michael Sneed, "Loyola President Proves to be Sister Jean's Guard- ian Angel," Chicago Sun Times, 3/24/18, viewed at https://chicago. suntimes.com/news/loyola-president-proves-to-be-sister-jeans-guardian- angel/ on 10/19/18.

4   "Sr. Jean Dolores Schmidt, BVM: A Living Legend at Loyola Uni- versity Chicago," viewed at the Jesuit Web Site at http://jesuits.org/ story?TN=PROJECT-20160307015136 on 3/28/18.

5   Loyola University Chicago upset Cincinnati 60-58 in overtime and be- came the 1963 National Basketball Champions.

6   Sat out the season per NCAA rules after transferring from the University of New Mexico.

7   The PGA of America in honor of famed British golfer Harry Vardon, awards the Vardon Trophy annually to the touring professional with the lowest adjusted scoring average. It is based on a minimum of 60 rounds, with no incomplete rounds, in events co-sponsored or designated by the PGA TOUR.

8   Al Geiberger was the first.

9   Sports Faith International is an initiative that honors athletes and others who lead exemplary lives. The author is Chairman.

10 See the ESPN Sport Century site at http://static.espn.go.com/sportscen- tury/athletes.html .

11 Cousy's inspirational story is in our second Sports and Faith Series book, *Sports and Faith: More Stories of the Devoted and Devout.*

12 Sports Faith International is an initiative that honors athletes and others who lead exemplary lives. The author is Chairman.

13 Facts used in the biography come from the Holy Cross website.

14 I included Coach Gordon's story in *Sports and Faith: Stories of the Devoted and the Devout* and mentioned him in *Sports and Faith: More Stories of the Devoted and the Devout* and *Pilgrimage.*

15 Lou Malnati's Pizzeria opened in Lawndale in 1995 to help rejuvenate the neighborhood. The restaurant chain has 50 locations in the Chicago area right now and has two more in Phoenix.

16 Barry Michaels, "Who is the Curé of Ars? St. John Vianney was patron of the Year for Priests," *The Catholic Answer*, Our Sunday Visitor, 10/12/09.

[17] "Napoleon," The Soldier's Life, PBS, viewed at http://www.pbs.org/empires/napoleon/n_war/soldier/page_1.html on April 5, 2018.

[18] Benson bought the New Orleans Hornets and renamed them the New Orleans Pelicans.

[19] Dag Hammarskjold died in a plane crash.

[20] Common reference to romantic figure as in Zorro.

[21] Some have suggested that she may have learned to read and write when she was incarcerated during her trial.

[22] Dauphin was a name used to identify the heir apparent in France. Dauphin is the French spelling for "dolphin" that is used on the Dauphin's coat of arms.

[23] Father John Vann (Ed.), *Lives of the Saints* (NY, John J. Crawley & Co., 1954) 301.

[24] Father John Vann (Ed.), *Lives of the Saints* (NY, John J. Crawley & Co., 1954)302.

[25] The Cardinals were originally the Chicago Cardinals, moved to St. Louis and then to Arizona.

[26] It should be noted that the Staley Company had a long history of success before it sold out to Tate and Lyle in the mid-1980s. The principle purchase was reported in the news at $1.42 Billion.

[27] Some of this material was taken from Patrick McCaskey's eBook called *Papa Bear and the Chicago Bears Winning Ways*.

[28] This section is based on material from *Pillars of the NFL: Coaches Who Have Won Three or More Championships* by Patrick McCaskey.

[29] Warren Brown, *Win, Lose or Draw*, (New York: G.P. Putnam's Sons, 1947) 269.

[30] I use this at some of my presentations. People who know me well would say it is vintage Pat McCaskey.

[31] Bacterial infection of the skin that could be serious at the time. .

[32] Pro Football Hall of Fame biography viewed at http://www.profootball-hof.com/players/mike-ditka/ on June 21, 2018.

[33] Buddy Young was a diminutive college and NFL athlete who became the first African American executive in the NFL.

[34] Father John Vann (Ed.), *Lives of the Saints* (NY, John J. Crawley & Co., 1954)34.

[35] See https://www.catholic.org/saints/saint.php?saint_id=28, http://www.newmanconnection.com/faith/saint/saint-blaise.

[36] These sayings are attributed to these coaches; they are not necessarily quotes and may not be original to the coach.

37   Billy Watkins, "Put me in God, I am Ready Pray," Clarion Ledger, viewed at https://www.clarionledger.com/story/magnolia/2017/11/02/mississippi-state-chicago-cubs-burke-masters-home-run-college-world-series-catholic-charities/823064001/ on November 2, 2017.

38   Masters's blog: https://frburke23.wordpress.com/

39   Sports Faith International is an initiative that honors athletes, coaches, and others in sports who lead exemplary lives. The author is Chairman of this organization.

40   Patristics is a branch of Christian theology that focuses on the lives, writings, and doctrines of the early Christian theologians.

41   A more detailed biography of Tom Monaghan was provided in *Sports and Faith: More Stories of the Devoted and the Devout* by Patrick McCaskey.

42   Father John Vann (Ed.), *Lives of the Saints* (NY: John J. Crawley & Co., 1954)28-29.

43   Nagurski's Wheaties box is an illustrated biographical montage like those you used to see in the newspapers—several drawn images of different sizes with captioned descriptions that are hand drawn rather than typeset.

44   Beth Gorr, *Bear Memories: The Chicago-Green Bay Rivalry* (Chicago, Arcadia, 2005) 115.

45   "El Camino de Santiago de Compostela" translated in English is the way of Saint James in the field of stars.

46   *Guideposts for the Spirit: Stories of Changed Lives*, ed. Peggy Schaffer (Nashville: Ideals Publications, 2003) 13.

47   From Longfellow's "A Psalm of Life."

48   Brady Halbmaier and Noah Brown, "Roberts Suits Up for Last Game as Tommies Win Portion of MIAC Title," *TommieMedia* viewed at https://www.tommiemedia.com/news/roberts-suits-up-for-last-game-as-tommies-win-portion-of-miac-title/ on 2/27/18.

49   Jostens is an American manufacturer of memorabilia including Jewelry such as the Super Bowl rings.

50   Loyola Academy web site viewed at https://www.goramblers.org/page/news-detail?pk=1009214 on May 22, 2018.

51   Discussed in Amato's acceptance speed at SFI 2018 induction banquet, also see video Frank Amato, "I'll Always be a Coach," Mike Lowe reporting viewed at https://www.youtube.com/watch?v=nn-WZEZ2My8 viewed on May 22, 2018.

52   Rosnat is mentioned in many places as a special place of learning, but scholars cannot agree on its early location.

53 There are nettles that irritate the skin—often called Ireland's poison ivy. They are also plants that offer certain medicinal qualities and have been used in soups.

54 *Topographia Hiberniae* is an account of the landscape and people of Ireland written by Gerald of Wales around 1188. It includes an account of Saint Kevin and the Blackbird.

55 Heaney's poem can be seen on various internet sites read by himself and others. The author is a great fan of Heaney's work.

56 Shane Newell, "Temecula Quarterback Gets Prosthetic Leg from NFL Quarterback Drew Brees," *Whittier Daily News*, May 17, 2018 viewed at https://www.whittierdailynews.com/2018/05/17/temecula-quarterback-gets-prosthetic-leg-from-nfl-quarterback-drew-brees/ on June 5, 2018.

57 National Shrine of Saint Jude has information on Danny Thomas: www.shrineofstjude.org/site/PageServer?pagename=ssj_jude_danny_thomas taken from an out-of-print book called *How St. Jude Came to Chicago* by John Kuenster published by Claretian Publications, but is currently out of print.

58 Summary information on Danny Thomas and his history with the St. Jude organization can be found at https://www.stjude.org/about-st-jude/history/how-we-began.html

59 The Indiana Football Hall of Fame site viewed at www.indiana-football.org/?q=node/414 on May 22, 2018.

60 Ellin Mackay's Irish American family had come from great poverty to America and achieved tremendous wealth. Mackay's grandfather and his partners discovered the Comstock Lode, the single largest silver lode that is estimated to have yielded $190 million in ore. See "A Jazz Age Love Story" from Irish American at http://irishamerica.com/2013/09/a-jazz-age-love-story/ .

61 The author was present at ceremonies celebrating the construction of the Center and spoke to the media.

62 *A Lynching in the Heartland*, James H. Madison, Palgram Macmillan, New York, 2003, p. 107

63 Books include James Cameron's *A Time of Terror: A Survivor's Story*; Cynthia Carr's *Our Town: A Heartland Lynching, A Haunted Town* and *the Hidden History of White America*; and James H. Madison's *A Lynching in the Heartland: Race and Memory in American*. Many articles have been written on the event and James Cameron's life and legacy.

64 "Message of Rosary priest has resonance for our times." The Irish Times, January 6, 2009, viewed at https://www.irishtimes.com/opinion/message-of-rosary-priest-has-resonance-for-our-times-1.1232454 on 2/8/18.

65 "Anti-Communist cardinal and 'Rosary Priest' declared venerable," Catholic Herald, December 17, 2017, viewed at http://www.catholicherald.co.uk/news/2017/12/19/anti-communist-cardinal-and-rosary-priest-declared-venerable/ on 2/8/18.

66 Olympic Ice Dancers whose gold-medal performance in 1984 to Bolero is considered a perfect artistic performance.

67 Some scholars believe that Pheidippides was a soldier who ran from the Athenians to Sparta to seek aid before the battle of Marathon against the Persians occurred. This would mean that the runner announcing the victory after the battle is unknown.

68 If you watch the Payton highlights films, each clip ends right when he is tackled. This is a shame because how he would spring up after a tackle was often as fun to watch.

69 Paul M. Pyrma, *Coaches of Chicago: Inspiring Stories about Leadership and Life*, (Rolling Meadows, IL, Windy City Publishers, 2014).

70 "St. John's Bill Wennington to be Inducted into Quebec Sports Hall of Fame," St. John's, The Official Home Page of St. John's University Athletics, viewed at https://redstormsports.com/news/2011/10/5/St_John_s_Bill_Wennington_To_Be_Inducted_Into_Quebec_Sports_Hall_of_Fame.aspx on October 19, 2018.

71 Dominican site http://www.op.org/en/content/st-dominic viewed on 6/1/18.

72 This community would become organized in the future was established quickly to meet the needs of the women in 1206. It is from this community that other communities came. For an example see the Adrian Dominican site at: the http://www.adriandominicans.org/OurStory/AWalkThroughHistory.aspx

73 Dominica Friars Foundation website viewed at https://dominicanfriars.org/about/our-mission/ on 2/18/18.

74 For more on this, see the Domincan web site Dominicana of the Dominican student brothers of the St. Joseph Province of the Order of Preachers at https://www.dominicanajournal.org/dominics-rule/ Also see information from the English Dominican site at www.dominicanajournal.org/dominics-rule/

75 Dominican Central Province website at viewed at http://opcentral.org/about-us/our-history/ on 2/18/18.

76 Sister Mary Faith Schuster, *The Meaning of the Mountain* (Baltimore: Helicon Press, 1963) 3.

77 Chicago Archdiocese site on Father Tolton at http://www.toltoncanonization.org/biography/biography.html viewed on 6/2/18.

78 See more on the Tolton Icon, which is sold to benefit the canonization effort, https://trinity-icons.myshopify.com/collections/classic-icons/products/father-tolton

79 See the author's book *Pilgrimage*, published by Sporting Chance Press for a review of the great pilgrimage sites.

80 Father John Vann (Ed.), *Lives of the Saints* (NY: John J. Crawley & Co., 1954) 419-420. Scholars have different opinions of St. Vincent's experiences as a slave, but much of his work that followed could be described as both a logical and inspired outcome of such an experience.

81 Many Religious orders of women have followed based in some ways on the Daughters of Charity and are often called Sisters of Charity. For example, Saint Elizabeth Ann Seton started the Sisters of Charity of Saint Joseph based on the rules written by St. Vincent de Paul for the Daughters of Charity.

82 See the US Society Facebook page at https://www.facebook.com/National-Council-of-the-United-States-Society-of-St-Vincent-de-Paul-186921794657204/

83 Charlestown has since gentrified to where a single floor of an old frame house in Long's old neighborhood now serves as a condominium unit that often sells for well over half a million dollars.

84 Long shares his sentiments on football in *Football for Dummies* co-authored with fellow FOX associate, John Czarnecki and published over several editions by John Wiley.

85 Paul Zimmerman, "The Long Way Up," Sports Illustrated Vault, July 22, 1985, viewed at http://www.si.com/vault/1985/07/22/620587/the-long-way-up on July 10, 2014.

86 John Underwood, "Running is Such Sweet Torture," *Sports Illustrated*, June 22, 1964, viewed from *Sports Illustrated* Vault site, at https://www.si.com/vault/1964/06/22/608708/running-is-such-sweet-torture on June 8, 2018.

87 Creamer, Robert, "From Humdrum To Well-done In One Easy Mile," *Sports Illustrated*, February 24, 1964.

88 Rather than the home of a single hermit, a hermitage at this time was a religious settlement of a community that would live in seclusion.

89 After College at Kansas, Lawson would go on to play for the Bengals, Vikings, and 49ers.

90 Chamberlin's football life is examined in *Pillars of the NFL: Coaches Who Have Won Three or More Championships*, Patrick McCaskey, Sporting Chance Press, 2014.

91 Wally Provost, "War Interrupts Gridiron Exploits," *Omaha World Herald*, September 2, 1964, p. 27.

92   Catholic Answers viewed on June 12. 2018 at https://www.catholic.com/encyclopedia/twelve-apostles-of-erin-the

93   Red Smith, "The Better Part of Frank's Valor," *New York Times*, August 1, 1977, p. 28.

94   The Jugglers is the Notre Dame Prep Theater Troupe.

95   The video has over 600,000 hits.

96   Father John Vann (Ed.), *Lives of the Saints* (NY: John J. Crawley & Co., 1954)120-121.

97   The Feast day of the Chair of Saint Peter is February 22. Legatus is an organization of wealthy Catholic business leaders.

98   Feast day of the Transfiguration is August 6.

99   Saint Anthony of Egypt Feast Day is January 17.

100   The author is Chairman of WSFI mentioned in poem. The feast of the Immaculate Conception is December 8.

101   Feast day of Saint Margaret of Scotland is November 16.

102   Feast day of Saint John the Baptist is June 24.

103   Feast day of Saint Bartholomew-Nathanael is August 24.

104   The feast day of Saint George is April 23. Saint George is patron saint of England.

105   Feast day is April 30.

– Photo and Illustration Credits –

All photographs are reproduced with permission (unless public domain).

Page	Photo Description	Source
Cover	Sister Jean Dolores Schmidt. BVM	Steve Woltmann/Loyola University Chicago Athletics
xvi	Sister Jean and Team in Prayer	Steve Woltmann/Loyola University Chicago Athletics
14	Wayne Gordon .	Lawndale Community Church
24	Saint John Vianney Courtyard of the house where saint lived from 1818-59. Behind is dome of the new Basilica where the saint's body is enshrined, next to the brick tower of the old parish church of Ars.	Fr. Lawrence Lew, O.P. Creative Commons (CC BY-NC-ND 2.0) See https://www.flickr.com/photos/paullew/19658060654/
26	George Halas Illustration	©William Potter
27	Bears Helmet	Daniel Norris
30	Oswald Chambers Family	Oswald Chambers Papers (SC/122), Special Collections, Buswell Library, Wheaton College (IL).
46	Westminster Cathedral mosaic of St Joan is by W. C. Symons and commissioned by Catholic Women's League in 1910.	Fr. Lawrence Lew, O.P. Creative Commons (CC BY-NC-ND 2.0) See https://www.flickr.com/photos/paullew/7301142176/
50	Shakespeare painting associated with John Taylor	Wikimedia Commons (Public Domain) from National Portrait Gallery of London
53	George Halas received the Sword of Loyola	Courtesy of Loyola University of Chicago Archives and Special Collections
68	Saint Blaise painting in the Dominican priory church in Dubrovnik.	Fr. Lawrence Lew, O.P. Creative Commons (CC BY-NC-ND 2.0) See https://www.flickr.com/photos/paullew/2241688061/

Page	Photo Description	Source
70	14 Holy Helpers painting in former church of the Augustinians, St Maurice in Fribourg, Holy Helpers were miracle-working saints associated with the alleviation of diseases and disasters--extremely popular in the Middle Ages.	Fr. Lawrence Lew, O.P. Creative Commons (CC BY-NC-ND 2.0) See https://www.flickr.com/photos/paullew/20872701129/
72	Guy Chamberlin Illustration	©William Potter
75	Father Burke Masters, Chaplain of the Cubs with Manager Joe Maddon	Father Burke Masters
88	Saint Lucy Feast Day celebration in Sweden	Photo by Fredrik L. Magnusson from Wikimedia Commons, (CC by 2.0)
91	Pillars of the NFL: Coaches Who Have Won Three or More Championships	Daniel Norris
96	Nagurski Wheaties Box Image	General Mills
108	Frank Amato Photo	Loyola Academy
115	Saint Kevin and the Blackbird Illustration	©Curt Rabinak
118	Sports and Faith I book	Daniel Norris
121	Frank Faunce and Son, Retired U.S. Army Colonel Frank Faunce	Retired U.S. Army Colonel Frank Faunce
126	Drew Brees and Alex Ruiz	Challenged Athletes Foundation
135	Irving Berlin	Wikimedia Commons, Public Domain
147	Bears Helmet	Daniel Norris
150	Patrick McCaskey of Notre Dame Prep	Notre Dame Prep (Niles)
164	Father Lawrence Lew at Saint Dominic's Birthplace. In the crypt of the nuns' church in Caleruega, Spain.	Fr. Lawrence Lew, O.P. Creative Commons (CC BY-NC-ND 2.0) See https://www.flickr.com/photos/paullew/3777374424/

Page	Photo Description	Source
168	Howard Cosell	Wikimedia Commons, Public Domain, originally created as publicity photo for Monday Night Football
170	Jim Finks, quarterback of the Pittsburgh Steelers of the National Football League, demonstrates his passing grip for Sister Mary Jonatha of the Sisters of Mercy Order, Rochester, N.Y., while in training at St. Bonaventure College at Olean, New York on July 28, 1955. (AP Photo/Walter Stein)	Associated Press
177	Icon of Father Augustus Tolton	Commissioned by Bishop Perry, created by Chicago iconographer, Joseph Malham of Trinity Icons. See https://trinity-icons.myshopify.com/collections/classic-icons/products/father-tolton
187	Chicago Bears Helmet	Daniel Norris
190	Chicago Bears Mug	Daniel Norris
194	Tom O'Hara Illustration	©William Potter
197	Stained glass window of Saint Anthony from St Casimir's parish in Baltimore, MD.	Fr. Lawrence Lew, O.P. Creative Commons (CC BY-NC-ND 2.0) See https://www.flickr.com/photos/paullew/27647763295/
210	Spartan Stadium Portsmouth, Ohio	Public Domain.
212	Saint Patrick's Cathedral New York	Fr. Lawrence Lew, O.P. Creative Commons (CC BY-NC-ND 2.0) See https://www.flickr.com/photos/paullew/21709344893/
218	Patrick McCaskey Notre Dame Prep	Notre Dame Prep (Niles)
226	Father Kyle Manno	Father Kyle Manno
234	Chicago Bears Helmet	Daniel Norris
238	Matthew, Basilica of Saint Elizabeth Ann Seton, Emmitsburg, MD	Fr. Lawrence Lew, O.P. Creative Commons (CC BY-NC-ND 2.0) See https://www.flickr.com/photos/paullew/37219211341/

Page	Photo Description	Source
255	Mark, Basilica of Saint Elizabeth Ann Seton, Emmitsburg, MD	Fr. Lawrence Lew, O.P. Creative Commons (CC BY-NC-ND 2.0) See https://www.flickr.com/photos/paullew/34106106752/
266	Luke, Basilica of Saint Elizabeth Ann Seton, Emmitsburg, MD	Fr. Lawrence Lew, O.P. Creative Commons (CC BY-NC-ND 2.0) See https://www.flickr.com/photos/paullew/37061268364/
273	John, Basilica of Saint Elizabeth Ann Seton, Emmitsburg, MD	Fr. Lawrence Lew, O.P. Creative Commons (CC BY-NC-ND 2.0)

– INDEX –